THE USBORNE BOOK OF
WORLD
HISTORY

Dr Anne Millard and Patricia Vanags

Designed by Graham Round

Illustrated by Joseph McEwan

Edited by Jenny Tyler

and Fiona Patchett

CONTENTS

About this book

SW

This book is an introduction to world history from the first
civilisations to the early 20th century. It uses clear and
simple language to trace the major developments in the
history of the world. Short, visual chapters introduce famous
figures, big battles and important discoveries. There are also
many fascinating facts about everyday life, along with
explanations of how archaeological evidence is used to find
out about the past. Important dates are shown in boxes for
quick reference. Time charts and maps make it easy to see
when and where things happened. This book does not
attempt to be a comprehensive account of the history of
the world, but it provides an excellent starting point.

Digging up History

We find out about peoples of the past by looking at the remains of things they left behind them and reading things they wrote. Digging up these remains is called archaeology.

The exact position of objects in the ground is very important. Modern archaeologists work with great care and patience, digging their site in sections and recording each find, however small.

Buried cities

A site may be inhabited for thousands of years. New houses are built on the ruins of the old rubbish piles. Gradually a mound or "tell" is formed. Start reading from the bottom of the page to find out how a tell formed.

After a capture, the city was burnt.

1250BC. More weapons appeared as the situation with neighbours got worse. The city was captured.

Iron arrowhead
Spear
Unburied body

Ancient writing

The Rosetta Stone with text in Greek and Ancient Egyptian.

Scholars spend years working out forgotten languages. This tablet was a lucky find. Its text was written in two languages, one of which was already known.

Carved stone relief from wall
Carved ivory decoration from furniture
Luxury goods of silver and gold

1500BC to 1250BC. The town grew into a city and became wealthy from foreign trade. It now needed huge defences against jealous neighbours.

Painting from house or temple wall
Local pottery

2000BC to 1500BC. Nomads arrived and were gradually and peacefully absorbed into the community. Arts, crafts and learning flourished.

Town wall of huge stones
Tablet with picture writing

3000BC to 2000BC. The village became a town. A defensive wall was built. The inhabitants began to make pottery and use copper and gold. They also began to write.

Copper fish hook
Carved stone statue

Human skull
Mud brick huts
Stamp seal
Fragment of woven cloth

6000BC to 3000BC. Early farmers settled down and built small huts. They had few possessions.

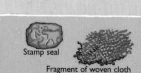
Flint tools
Animal bones

Stone Age people camped here. They left flint tools and bones.

The letters BC mean "Before Christ". Dates with BC next to them are numbers of years before the birth of Christ. All these dates are approximate.

The tell in this picture has been made up to give you an idea of how archaeologists can dig down through history. No real mound would have such flat, regular layers. The objects are not drawn to scale.

Layer of sand and dirt

Iron axe of invader

Unburied bodies

Citizens' spears

Monumental gateway

Foreign pottery

Stone statue

Piles of tablets covered with text

Local pottery

Bronze sword

Copper spear head

Gold necklace

Burial of nomad

Clay tablet with writing

Pottery introduced by new-comers

Well-built huts

Bead necklace

Pottery jar

Bits of first pottery

Stone jar

Stone figure of a goddess

Wooden bowl

Bones of tamed animals

Animal tusk

Human jawbone

Radiocarbon dating

A substance called radioactive carbon or C14, leaves plants when they die. Scientists measure C14 to find out when plants died.

Tree-ring dating

Every year a tree adds a ring round its trunk. It is possible to make a chart of rings which goes back for centuries and use it for dating old wood.

Putting pieces together

Every fragment found on a dig had to be numbered and recorded, so this chair could be reconstructed.

3

The First Settlers

Around 10,000BC, our ancestors gathered plants, and hunted and fished for food. They were nomads, wandering from place to place after the herds they hunted. A good supply of food meant they could settle in one place for a while.

Rush basket

Drying skin

Leather skirt

Wolf-tooth necklace

Fishing net

Cleaning animal skin with flint scraper

Carving an antler

Stone tools

Some Stone Age people made homes in the caves of northern Europe. They made tools from stone, wood and bone, and clothes from animal skins.

The children were told stories of the past by the old people of the tribe. Their fathers hunted and fished and their mothers gathered berries and plants.

Learning to farm

1. Gradually people realized that seeds dropped on the ground grew into plants. They began to plant seeds specially.

2. They chose the best seeds and got a bigger harvest. This was more reliable than hunting, so people settled down to farm.

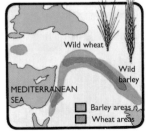

Wild wheat

Wild barley

MEDITERRANEAN SEA

Barley areas
Wheat areas

3. This discovery must have taken place in the Middle East where ancestors of wheat and barley plants grew wild.

4

Taming animals

Building houses

People began to tame animals. They tamed sheep and goats first and then cattle, pigs and donkeys. This meant they had a supply of meat, milk, wool and animals for carrying loads.

People settled where the land was good for farming. If there were no caves nearby, they had to build homes from materials they found locally. They built a style of house to suit the climate.

New crafts

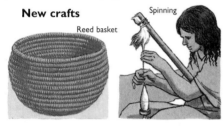

Reed basket

Spinning

Weaving

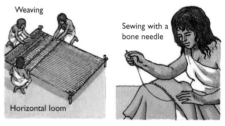

Sewing with a bone needle

Horizontal loom

Staying in one place gave people more spare time. They improved old skills, like weaving reeds into baskets and developed new ones like spinning and pottery. Pottery may have been discovered when a clay-lined basket accidentally fell in a fire.

With the wool from sheep and goats, people discovered how to spin, weave and make cloth. They learned to make linen cloth from the fibres of the flax plant. Needles made from bone were used to sew cloth together to make clothes.

Making a simple loom

Early pottery

Use a piece of card about 20cm x 12cm (8in. x 5in.). Cut triangles out of the ends to make "teeth". Wind wool round the card to make the "warp". Weave "weft" wool in and out of the warp.

Using metal

Pouring molten metal into mould to make axe-head

Melting the metal

Rough cooking pots were probably made by women. In some settlements, potters spent all day making better pots.

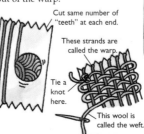

Cut same number of "teeth" at each end.

These strands are called the warp.

Tie a knot here.

This wool is called the weft.

People had been settled for thousands of years before they discovered how to use copper, silver, gold and then bronze.

5

THE FIRST CITIES: 8000BC to 5650BC

Jericho

Near the modern city of Jericho lie the remains of one of the oldest towns in the world.

A town grows

1. After 10,000BC a group of hunters, attracted by food and water, settled on the site which was to become Jericho.

*Cut-away wall

2. By about 8000BC, they were living in a village and probably farmed. They buried their dead under their houses.

3. The village grew into a town. To protect themselves against neighbours, they built a wall with towers and a ditch round it.

4. Local goods such as salt were traded for cowrie shells from the Red Sea, obsidian from Turkey and turquoise from Sinai.

Grinding corn

5. Jericho must have been captured. By 7000BC, the people who lived there built rectangular houses instead of round ones.

Bricks drying in the sun

Finger holes

6. Houses were built of mud bricks, moulded by hand and left to dry in the sun. This kind of brick is still used in dry places.

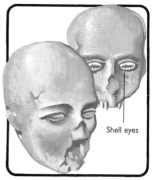

Shell eyes

7. Skulls with faces modelled in plaster were dug up at Jericho. Scholars think they were made to show respect for the dead.

Çatal Hüyük

Of all the ancient settlements found so far, the largest is Çatal Hüyük (pronounced Chatal Hooyuk). Excavations show that it flourished between 6500BC and 5650BC.

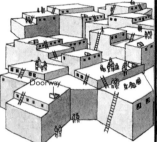

The houses were one storey high. People entered them by climbing a ladder and crawling through a hole in the roof. This meant it was difficult for enemies to get in.

Obsidian mirror

Steps to doorway

Obsidian daggers

Carved wooden dish

Sleeping platform (the dead were buried under here.)

Stove

Houses had one main room. Benches and sleeping platforms were built in to the walls. Woven mats covered the floor. The people used the obsidian, or volcanic glass, found nearby for making daggers and mirrors and traded them for flint and shells.

Statue of Çatal Hüyük goddess

Real horns

The people worshipped a goddess who is shown as a girl, a mother or an old woman. They worshipped a god whose sacred animal was a bull.

Many shrines have been found at Çatal Hüyük. Their walls were brightly painted with religious scenes and decorated with plaster bulls' heads.

Wall paintings suggest that some priestesses dressed as vultures and conducted rituals. Human skulls were found in baskets below the bulls' heads.

The first great civilisation

Some 7,000 years ago, farmers began to settle in the area between the Euphrates and Tigris rivers. This area was later called "Mesopotamia" by the Ancient Greeks, which means "The land between two rivers". It is roughly where Iraq is now. Life was hard there. The weather was hot and dry and the rivers flooded, but the land was fertile when properly looked after. Gradually, in the south, in the land of Sumer, a great civilisation grew up.

Map of Sumer

The land of Sumer where the Sumerians lived was in the southern part of Mesopotamia. The land near the Persian Gulf was very marshy and difficult to farm, but there were plenty of fish and wild fowl there for the settlers to eat.

 City-states

Marshy land

To the north of Sumer, was the land which later became called Akkad.

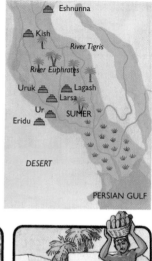

1. Sumer had no stone or tall trees for building. Houses were built with reeds. People still build with reeds there today.

2. The two rivers flooded in early summer. The Sumerians built irrigation canals to water their fields and drain the land.

3. Later, they built houses of sun-dried mud bricks. These buildings kept them cool in summer and warm in winter.

4. Every village was protected by a god or goddess who lived in a temple. The priests of the temple became very powerful.

5. Sumerian villages grew into huge, walled, self-governing city-states, with a temple at the centre and farmland all around.

6. Sometimes one city-state conquered another, but no-one made himself ruler of all of Sumer, let alone Mesopotamia.

How we know

An inlaid box, called the "Battle Standard", was found at Ur. It shows scenes of life in peacetime on one side and scenes of war on the other.

This shows what Sumerian warriors, weapons and chariots looked like. Sumerians did not have horses, so chariots were pulled by donkeys or asses.

We can get an idea of what Sumerians looked like and what they wore from statues found in temples. Nobles or priests seem to have shaved their heads.

The ziggurat of Ur

Holy shrine where the patron god of the city had one of his dwelling places

Temple staff lived in these houses.

This ziggurat is thought to have been about 21 metres high.

A religious procession on its way to the temple

By about 2000BC, temples had developed into huge temple-towers, called ziggurats, like this one at Ur. The temples employed large numbers of craftsmen, labourers and scribes.

9

The invention of writing

This stone vase records offerings made to the goddess Inanna at Ur.

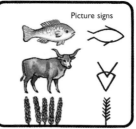

Picture signs

1. Temples collected gifts for the gods and goddesses and handed out goods as payment. A system of account-keeping was needed.

2. They drew sketches of objects using a flattened pieced of clay and a reed pen. This is the earliest form of writing.

3. At first, pictures were drawn on wet clay. The clay was dried in the sun or baked in a kiln to make it into a hard tablet.

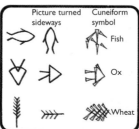

Picture turned sideways	Cuneiform symbol	
		Fish
		Ox
		Wheat

4. Later, scribes found it was easier to draw signs sideways. The pictures became less like the objects they represented.

5. The reed pen made the pictures look wedge-shaped. We call this writing cuneiform, meaning "wedge-shaped".

6. Signs were adapted and used together so other words could be built up and sentences formed to express ideas.

Sumerian schools

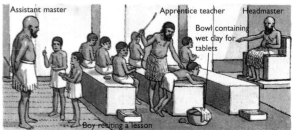

Assistant master · Apprentice teacher · Headmaster · Bowl containing wet clay for tablets · Boy reciting a lesson

Those who could afford to, sent their sons to school. School began very early. The boys had to work very hard.

Reading, writing and arithmetic were taught. Discipline was very strict. Boys were beaten for not doing their lessons well.

One Sumerian story tells of a boy getting a good report by persuading his father to give the master a gift.

A Sumerian market

Sumer had no metal, stone or timber so all these things had to be imported from other countries.

This scribe checks that the right amount of goods is being unloaded.

Writing made the business of buying and selling in markets much easier. If a dispute arose over a deal, the written contract could be checked.

This trader can keep an account of the amount he is owed for his skins.

Sealing a contract with a cylinder seal

People who could not write hired public scribes to write letters for them.

Cylinder seals

Carved stone seal   Impression of seal in clay

Instead of signing their names, Sumerians rolled cylinder seals across wet clay. No seals were alike, so the owner could be identified.

Measuring and calculating

Scribes measured land to see how much tax farmers had to pay. Fields were divided into squares which were counted.

Sumerians counted using a system like ours, based on the unit 10, and another based on the unit 60, still used to measure time.

Your own picture writing

You can make picture signs with a sharp pencil on a flattened piece of plasticine. You could make up a system of picture writing and use it to write messages to your friends.

This message could mean "meet me by the tree, on the corner of the football field, at 3 o'clock, to go fishing".

11

Daily life

The Sumerians thought that their city-states were owned by the local gods and goddesses. They divided the land into three parts and farmed one part of it for the gods. This produce was stored and used in times of famine or traded for foreign goods.

The second part of the land produced food for priests and temple staff. The third was hired by citizens to grow food for themselves. They paid rent with some of the crop.

A nobleman at home

The king ran the city-state on behalf of the gods, with the help of priests, scribes and nobles. Some of these were very rich and enjoyed a good life.

This gaming board comes from one of the royal graves of Ur. The rules are not known, though recently, a way of playing it has been worked out.

A rich merchant's house

Bedroom

Servant girl

Master's bedroom

Wash bowl and jug

Ladles and strainers

Kitchen

To lavatory

Servants' room

Water jars

Spinning

Fire for cooking　　Reed mat

Built-in mud bench

Archaeologists found large, two-storey houses, like this one, at Ur. They were built of mud bricks round open courtyards. They had

lavatories and drains, but not baths. Houses like this probably belonged to wealthy merchants, but whose status was beneath that of the priests and nobles.

Most ordinary Sumerians lived in small, one-storey houses built of mud bricks. Windows, if they had them, were small to keep out the heat and cold.

Farming in Sumer

The wealth of Sumer came from its rich farming land. Farmers had to work hard to keep the fields watered and the irrigation canals in good repair.

Irrigation canal

Farmhouse

Cow byre

Churning milk to make butter

Straining milk

Milking

Sowing seed

Oxen, which were used for ploughing, were a farmer's most treasured possession.

The first wheels

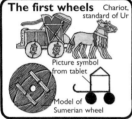

Chariot, standard of Ur

Picture symbol from tablet

Model of Sumerian wheel

The first evidence of wheels comes from Sumer. Sumerian wheels were made from three pieces of wood, lashed together.

Metalwork

Sumerian metalsmiths were skilled workers in gold, silver and copper. The things they made were expensive as all Sumer's metal was imported.

Potters at work

Clay being mixed

Kilns

Pots drying out before baking

Potter's wheel

Though stone and wood were scarce in Sumer, there was plenty of mud and clay which could be used to make pottery. So much pottery was needed that skilled potters worked full time.

The royal graves of Ur

This gold jewellery comes from one of the royal graves of Ur. These graves contain the skeletons of dozens of people who appear to have committed suicide in order to follow the graves' owners to another world.

Key dates

5000	Early farming communities using pottery, living in northern Mesopotamia.
4000	Communities established in the south, in Sumer. The Ubaid period.
3300/2800	Rapid development of the civilisation of Sumer.
2750	The Royal Graves of Ur.
2700	**Gilgamesh** reigned at Uruk. 1st Dynasty (line of hereditary rulers) at Ur.
2500	2nd Dynasty at Ur.

Approximate BC dates

First settlers on the Nile

1. Thousands of years ago, the Sahara was a well-watered plain where wild animals lived. Stone Age people lived there too and hunted the animals.

2. Slowly the climate changed and the Sahara became a desert. People and animals had to search for a water supply. Some reached the land we call Egypt.

3. The valley of the River Nile was a marshy jungle where dangerous animals lived. The newcomers camped on the edges of the valley for safety.

4. Hunters learnt to tame animals rather than hunt them. They domesticated dogs, cattle, sheep, pigs, goats and donkeys.

5. The number of people grew and they were able to clear land near the river and build villages there. They found out how to plant seeds and grew wheat, barley and vegetables. They discovered how to spin, make pottery, weave flax to make linen clothes and use metals to make tools and weapons.

Before the inundation

During the inundation

6. Every July, flood waters burst the Nile's banks and soaked the hard, dry ground. The flood lasted several weeks and was called the inundation.

7. Ancient Egyptians discovered how to save enough flood water to last the year. They cut canals and ditches which stored the water and carried it to the fields.

Egypt becomes one land

The name "Narmer"

The god, Horus, helping Narmer

Defeated ruler of Lower Egypt

Beheaded enemies

King Narmer wearing his White Crown

King Narmer wearing the Red Crown

Gradually communities in the Nile Valley joined together. By 3200BC, Egypt had just two kings – one in Lower Egypt and one in Upper Egypt. Then they fought a battle which was won by Upper Egypt.

Here you can see the two sides of King Narmer's palette. The pictures carved on it show Narmer, King of Upper Egypt, defeating the King of Lower Egypt and claiming to be the king of the whole land.

A new capital was built for the united land at Memphis. As ruler of The Two Lands, the king wore the Double Crown. He also carried the Crook and Flail to show he was shepherd and defender of his people.

Double Crown

Crook and Flail

Map of Egypt

MEDITERRANEAN SEA

THE DELTA

• Sais • Tanis

SINAI

LOWER EGYPT

RED CROWN OF KING OF LOWER EGYPT

• Giza
• Sakkarah
Memphis

• Beni Hasan

• Amarna

River Nile

WHITE CROWN OF KING OF UPPER EGYPT

Aswam

Abydos •

VALLEY OF THE KINGS

• Thebes

NUBIA

• Edfu

• Aswam

In the north, Egypt widens into the Delta area. This map shows the borders between Upper and Lower Egypt before the country was united in about 3120BC.

The king's name

The Egyptians thought it rude to refer directly to the king, so they spoke of "The Great House". The Egyptian picture signs, or hieroglyphs, for this are pronounced "per-o". The word "pharoah" which we use for Egyptian kings comes from this.

Egyptian hieroglyphs for "per-o"

The farmers' year

1. Every July, the waters of the Nile began to rise. The land flooded and animals had to be moved onto higher ground.

2. By November, the water had gone down. The damp earth was broken up with sticks, ploughed and sown with seed.

3. Egypt has little rain during most of the year. The fields were watered with flood waters which had been stored in canals.

4. The crops grew during winter. Tax officials measured the crop and decided how much of it the farmer must pay as tax.

5. The crop was harvested in the spring. The farmer's family helped with this.

6. Cattle were used to separate the grain from the stalks. The grain was tossed so the husks would blow away.

7. The grain was stored in the granaries, in huge bins called silos. The scribes had the job of checking that none was stolen.

8. The irrigation canals and ditches then had to be repaired and made ready for the next flood.

9. In the inundation, some farmers worked on the pharoah's building projects. This was part of the tax they owed him.

Food and drink

It was the prayer of all Egyptians that, in the Next World, they would have all the good things to eat and drink that they had known in life.

The Nile provided much food. They used nets to trap wild ducks, geese and other water birds that lived in the reeds and also caught many kinds of fish.

Birds were also raised on farms where they were forcibly fattened for the table, like the stork in this picture. The eggs of these birds were eaten too.

Egypt had little good pasture, so cattle raised for meat were fattened in stalls. This wooden model of a cow stall came from an Egyptian tomb at Thebes.

Grapes were grown on trellises. To make them into wine, they were put into troughs and the juice trodden out. Treaders held ropes to stop them slipping.

Wine jars had inscriptions on them saying where the wine came from and when it was produced. These are often valuable as historical evidence.

Bread

Beer

Grain was ground into flour between stones. To make dough, flour was mixed with water.

Garlic or honey, were added to the dough. It was packed into clay pots and baked.

Some loaves were baked lightly, mixed with water and then sieved to make beer.

Beer needed straining before it was drunk. Pottery strainers were made for the purpose.

17

Tombs and life after death

Death of a nobleman

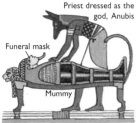

Priest dressed as the god, Anubis

Funeral mask

Mummy

Canopic jars

1. When, despite the efforts of the doctors and the prayers of the priests, an Egyptian noble died, his body was embalmed to prevent it from decaying.

2. The brain and internal organs were removed and placed in "canopic" jars. The body was treated with a substance called natron to help preserve it.

3. The body was wrapped in layers of linen bandages and a funeral mask put over its face. We often call a body embalmed like this, a "mummy".

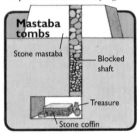

Mastaba tombs

Stone mastaba

Blocked shaft

Treasure

Stone coffin

In the Old Kingdom (2686 to 2181BC), noblemen were buried under rectangular stone tombs called mastabas. Some contained decorated rooms.

The pyramids

Kings of the Old and Middle Kingdoms of Egypt (2686 to 1633BC) were buried under huge stone pyramids. There are more than 30 pyramids in Egypt, but the most famous are the ones in Giza, shown here, where three kings and their chief queens were buried. Originally these pyramids were encased in gleaming white limestone, but this has now disappeared.

The sphinx

The sphinx, which guards the pyramids of Giza, was a form of the Egyptian sun god. Its face may be a likeness of Khafra.

Poor peoples' graves

Box of clothes

Oil jar

Wine jar

Mummy

Poor people were buried in holes in the sand. Relatives buried items for the dead person to use in the Next World.

The pyramid of Khafra (Greek name, Chephren)

The pyramid of Menkawre (Greek name, Mycerinus)

The pyramid of Khufu, who is often called by his Greek name Cheops. This is the Great Pyramid.

The queens' pyramids

4. Embalming took 70 days. Then the funeral took place. Mourners, priests and grave goods accompanied the coffin across the Nile to the tomb.

5. The last rites were performed at the tomb door. The "Opening of the Mouth" ceremony gave back to the dead person, the power to eat, breathe and move.

6. All that the dead man needed in the Next World was put in the burial chamber. The priests then left, sweeping away their footprints as they went.

Isis

Osiris, god of the dead

Thoth, scribe of the gods

Horus leading dead man

Dead man's heart

Anubis

The Egyptians believed the souls of the dead were ferried across a river into the Next World. Here they had to answer questions about their actions on Earth. Priests wrote the Book of the Dead, which told them what to say and do. In the presence of Osiris, god of the dead, their heart was weighed against a feather representing truth. If the scales balanced, the person went to eternal joy. If the heart was heavy with sin, a monster gobbled it up.

19

Building the pyramids

Casing of gleaming white limestone

The pyramids of Giza are one of the wonders of the world. They were built without machines. The men who built them were not slaves, but peasant farmers who worked for the king during the inundation and were paid for their service in food, oil and cloth. They probably hoped that by helping with the king's preparations for death, they would please the gods and be rewarded in the Next World.

Khufu's pyramid

The height of Khufu's pyramid is 148m (485ft)

When Khafra's pyramid is completed it will contain nearly 2,300,000 blocks of stone, like his father's.

Wooden poles are used to lever the blocks into place.

Blocks of stone are dragged on sledges from nearby quarries. Wheels are not used at all.

Chief architect

The blocks weigh an average of 2,300 kg.

Later, Khafra's pyramid will be finished, like his father's, with a layer of high quality white limestone. This will be brought from quarries across the Nile. The blocks will be put on rafts and floated across the river while it is in flood.

20

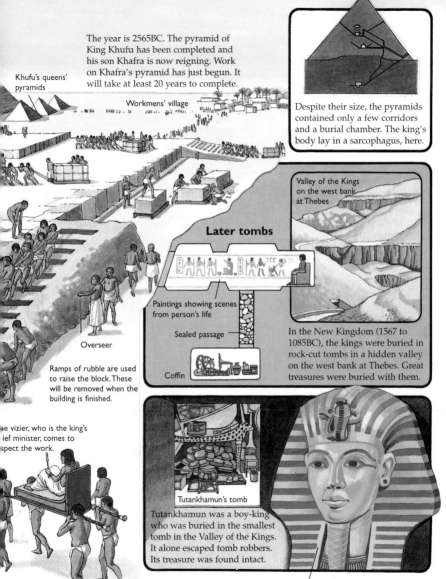

The year is 2565BC. The pyramid of King Khufu has been completed and his son Khafra is now reigning. Work on Khafra's pyramid has just begun. It will take at least 20 years to complete.

Khufu's queens' pyramids

Workmens' village

Despite their size, the pyramids contained only a few corridors and a burial chamber. The king's body lay in a sarcophagus, here.

Valley of the Kings on the west bank at Thebes

Later tombs

Paintings showing scenes from person's life

Sealed passage

Coffin

Overseer

Ramps of rubble are used to raise the block. These will be removed when the building is finished.

In the New Kingdom (1567 to 1085BC), the kings were buried in rock-cut tombs in a hidden valley on the west bank at Thebes. Great treasures were buried with them.

e vizier, who is the king's ief minister, comes to spect the work.

Tutankhamun's tomb

Tutankhamun was a boy-king who was buried in the smallest tomb in the Valley of the Kings. It alone escaped tomb robbers. Its treasure was found intact.

Tutankhamun's mask

21

Sport and leisure

Painted wooden pillars

These children are playing a kind of tug-of-war.

Young dancing girls

Wrestlers

Harp

This is the garden of a rich Egyptian. Singing, music and dancing were favourite entertainments. We have no written music from Ancient Egypt, but the words of some songs have survived, and some musical instruments.

Children's games

Children's basket of toys from a tomb

Ivory dog

Egyptian tomb paintings, like these, show us some of the games played by children, but they do not tell us the rules. They are often shown playing ball games. The balls they used were made of leather, stuffed with grain.

If a child died, toys were buried with him, like those in the basket above. Toys with moving parts were popular. This ivory hound opens and shuts its mouth as if to bark, when a rod underneath it is pressed.

Hunting on the Nile

Tame birds were held to attract the wild ones.

One of the most dangerous animals in Egypt was the hippopotamus. To hunt it, several skilled men were needed, armed with harpoons, spears, ropes and nets.

Water tournament

Egyptian noblemen hunted and fished in the marshes using small boats made of papyrus stems bound together. They speared fish and used throwing sticks to bring down birds.

Some had hunting cats, which were trained to retrieve the fallen birds. A man often took his family on these expeditions too and they had a picnic on their boat.

The object of this competition was to knock the crew of the rival boat into the water, one by one, without being toppled in yourself.

Egyptian cosmetics

Both men and women used cosmetics. Oils and perfumes were used on the skin, the lips were painted red, and green and grey kohl was used to outline the eyes. Kohl was made from finely ground minerals mixed with oil.

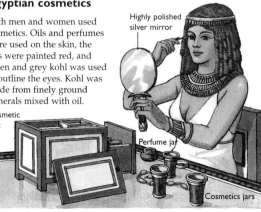

Highly polished silver mirror

Cosmetic box

Perfume jar

Cosmetics jars

Key dates

5000	First traces of farming communities in Egypt.
4000/3500	Farmers prospered, communities grew and united.
3118	Upper and Lower Egypt united by **Menes**, first king of Dynasty I.
2686	**The Old Kingdom**. Beginning of Dynasty III. Step pyramids built.
2613	Dynasty IV. Giza pyramids built.
2180	End of Old Kingdom. Time of civil war and anarchy called First Intermediate Period.
2040	Egypt reunited. **The Middle Kingdom**. A period of great prosperity during Dynasties XI to XIII.
1720	The Hyksos invaded. Second Intermediate Period.
1567	Egypt reunited and the Hyksos driven out.

Approximate BC dates

23

A great island civilisation

The descendants of the farmers who settled on the island of Crete were free from invasion for hundreds of years. This meant they could develop their own distinctive way of life.

We call the culture of the people of Crete "Minoan" after King Minos who is said to have ruled there. Many Minoan sites have been identified and excavated.

Houses

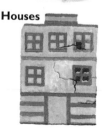

Small pieces of glazed pottery like this one were probably used to decorate furniture. They give an idea what Minoan town houses looked like.

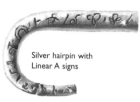

Silver hairpin with Linear A signs

1. The Minoans sometimes used a system of hieroglyphs, or picture signs, for writing. They also had a script called Linear A, which has not yet been deciphered.

3. This fresco shows a Cretan fisherman with his catch of fresh mackerel. As the people lived close to the sea, fish was an important part of their diet.

Frescoes

Houses and palaces were decorated with frescoes like these. A fresco is a picture painted on the plaster of a wall while the plaster is still damp.

2. Besides wheat, barley, vegetables and grapes, the farmers grew large quantities of olives. The olives in this picture were dug up on Crete and are 3,400 years old.

4. Bronze and pottery cooking pots have been found, but fish were probably grilled on sticks over a fire. Oil from crushed olives was used in cooking.

How to make a fresco

Plaster mixed with water

Big foil dish

When plaster is dry, remove it from dish.

Hook made from bent wire

To make a "fresco", mix some plaster of Paris. Pour it into a foil dish. When it is firm but damp, paint on it with water paints. You must work quickly.

The palace at Knossos

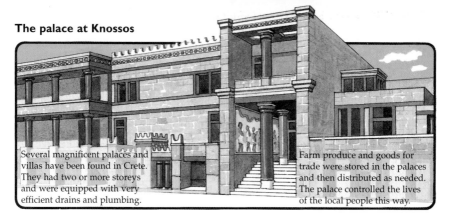

Several magnificent palaces and villas have been found in Crete. They had two or more storeys and were equipped with very efficient drains and plumbing.

Farm produce and goods for trade were stored in the palaces and then distributed as needed. The palace controlled the lives of the local people this way.

The rooms in Minoan palaces were covered with bright frescoes. This is one of the queen's rooms in the palace of Knossos.

These large jars are called pithoi. They once held grain, wine and olive oil in the storage rooms of the palace of Knossos. They were found during excavations in 1900.

This throne, found at Knossos, is the oldest in Europe still in place. The decorations were probably done by Myceneans who occupied the palace.

Life on Crete

Trade

The Cretans made beautiful pottery which is easy to identify. It has been found in lots of places, so we know the Cretans traded far afield.

Games and sports

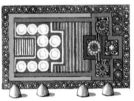

No-one knows the rules of the game once played on this board, called the royal gaming board. Dice seem to have been a popular game.

This picture of boys boxing is based on a fresco found on the wall of a buried house, on the nearby island of Thera. Each boy wears only one glove.

According to tradition the Cretans were daring sailors and successful traders. The sailors of the legendary King Minos were said to rule the Mediterranean Sea.

The Egyptians recorded the arrival of Cretan traders in their tombs. The Cretans are shown carrying objects similar to those that have actually been found on Minoan sites.

Frescoes and models show that Cretans enjoyed a dangerous sport called bull-leaping. Trained men and girls somersaulted between the horns of a charging bull. They worked in teams of three. One leaping, one catching and one ready for the next leap. This may have been a way of honouring the gods.

Religion and legend

Although they worshipped some gods, the leading role in Cretan religion was played by goddesses and their priestesses.

Gold and ivory statuette of a popular Cretan goddess

1. This picture, which is from a seal impression, shows the goddess who was Queen of the Animals, standing on her mountain. The building in the background may be a shrine.

3. The Double Axe was a religious symbol. It appears on frescoes and various objects. Actual axes have also been found. This one is made of gold.

2. Cretans probably enjoyed dancing for its own sake, but it was also a way of worship. One legend tells how the craftsman Daedalus made a special dance floor for the Princess Ariadne.

4. Legend says a monster, the Minotaur, lived on Crete. It was half bull and half man and lived in the Labyrinth. Theseus, the hero, found a way in and killed it.

The fall of Crete

Thera was a small, round island, near Crete. In about 1500BC, a huge volcano eruption blew much of the island away. The white area on the map shows the land that sank beneath the sea.

Houses were buried under a thick layer of lava and ash, which preserved their walls to an unusual height. Modern excavations are now revealing the houses, their frescoes and other contents.

Some people think ash falls and tidal waves from the eruption at Thera, damaged Crete so much it never recovered. Invaders from Greece ruled at Knossos, but Cretan glory was past.

Key dates

6000/5000	Farmers living in settled communities.
4000	Beginning of metalworking. Evidence of gradually increasing prosperity.
2500/1950	Early Minoan Period. Towns developing.
1950	Middle Minoan Period. First palaces built. Picture writing (hieroglyphs) in use.
1700	Late Minoan Period. Great wealth and art. Palaces expanded.
1500	Eruption on nearby island of Thera. The arrival of the Mycenaeans from Greece. Linear B writing in use.
1200	Many sites abandoned.

Approximate BC dates

Cities of Ancient India

As in Mesopotamia and Egypt, people were drawn to the Indus Valley because of the river. The river meant that there was good farming land and a steady supply of fish. Goods could be carried more easily by river than across land.

It was not known until 1921 that a great and ancient civilisation had once existed in the Indus Valley. Much has been learnt about its people since then, but there are still many puzzles to be solved, perhaps by further excavations.

River Indus
• Harappa
• Mohenjo-daro

INDIA

Very few statues of the Indus people have been found. This one may be a priest. Skeletons from Harappa show that most people died before they were 40.

Inside an Indus Valley house

The citizens of the Indus Valley cities lived in pleasant mud brick houses which were built around courtyards. In a rich man's house, like the one shown below, there was a well.

A street in Mohenjo-daro

Covered drain

Cities like Mohenjo-daro and Harappa were carefully planned with long, straight main streets linked by smaller lanes. Good drains ran down the main streets.

The houses had brick lavatories, connected to the main drains by chutes.

Flat roof

Bedrooms

Courtyard

Clay missiles

Mohenjo-daro was protected by brick walls and towers. Piles of large clay missiles lay behind the walls ready for use, perhaps, as ammunition for slings.

Mud brick walls
Well
Lavatory

Writing

Seals have been found which show the Indus people could write, but no-one today can read them. They were probably used to stamp the owner's name.

Make a stamp seal

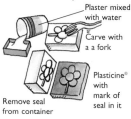

Plaster mixed with water

Carve with a a fork

Plasticine® with mark of seal in it

Remove seal from container

Mix plaster with water. Pour it into a small container. Let it dry, then carve pictures on it with a fork. Turn out seal. Use it to make your mark on a piece of plasticine®.

Granary at Mohenjo-daro

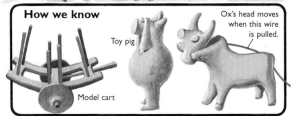

The granary was one of the most important buildings in the city. Farming was the chief source of wealth. The Indus people grew wheat, barley and vegetables and seem to have been the first people to grow cotton. Several other large buildings, including a great bath, have also been found.

How we know

Toy pig

Ox's head moves when this wire is pulled.

Model cart

These baked clay models are valuable archaeological evidence. They were probably toys, but give a good idea of what kind of carts people had and what their animals looked like.

Trade

Metal for statues was bought abroad. We know Indus people traded in Mesopotamia as their pottery has been found there.

The end of civilisation

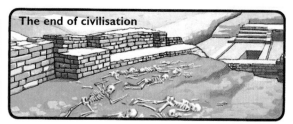

Excavations show that, by about 1700BC, Indus cities were less well-organized and poorer than before. The causes of this decline are not yet understood.

At Mohenjo-daro, remains of unburied bodies have been found. This suggests the city was destroyed by enemies, possibly Aryan people.

29

The rise of Babylon

Bronze head of Sargon

About 2370BC, Sargon appeared in Mesopotamia. He spoke Akkadian. He conquered and united the city-states of Mesopotamia for the first time.

One account of Sargon's life says he was found in a basket, floating on the river. He became cup-bearer to the king of the city of Kish, then overthrew him.

Sargon built a capital city called Akkad, but its site has never been identified. His empire lasted 200 years and was then overthrown.

Gutian tribesmen invaded Mesopotamia, but the rulers of Ur gained control. Amorite invaders began to arrive.

Babylon had an Amorite king called Hammurabi, who, in a series of brilliant wars, united all of Mesopotamia.

This carving shows Hammurabi being handed symbols of justice by a god. The law code he devised is carved below.

Hammurabi's laws

Hammurabi's laws seem harsh today. If a surgeon performed an operation that caused a death, his hand was cut off.

Another law said that if an architect built a house which collapsed and killed its owner, the architect was put to death.

Key dates

2371/2316	**Sargon** of Akkad.
2200	End of the Akkadian empire. Arrival of Gutian invaders.
2113	3rd Dynasty of Ur. Time when Ur ruled much of Mesopotamia.
2006	Overthrow of Ur. Cities of Isin and Larsa struggled for supremacy while Amorite invaders moved in.
1900	1st Dynasty of Babylon.
1972/1750	**Hammurabi** of Babylon.
1592	Babylon raided by Hittites from Anatolia, then taken over and ruled by tribes men called Kassites.

Approximate BC dates

Myths

The people of Mesopotamia had many gods and goddesses. Below are some of the stories they wrote about them.

Hammurabi made his god, Marduk, the most powerful god of Mesopotamia.

The priests told how Marduk had saved the world from the sea-monster, Tiamat. The victory was celebrated each year at the New Year festival.

The Mesopotamians thought the world was a flat. One story says Marduk created the world by building a reed raft on the waters and pouring dust on it.

The great flood

Once, the gods were angry with men, and they decided to destroy them in a great flood. They warned one good man, Ut-napishtim. He built a boat.

The flood came and all was destroyed except Ut-napishtim's boat, which came to rest on a mountain. The birds he sent out could find nowhere to settle.

Finally he sent out a raven and it did not return. The earth had begun to dry out. Ut-napishtim and his family thanked the gods for saving them.

Gilgamesh

Enkidu

Gilgamesh

Gilgamesh, king of Uruk, angered the gods. They sent Enkidu to destroy him, but the two became friends.

They had adventures, but Enkidu was killed. Afraid of death, Gilgamesh went to Ut-napishtim who had the secret of eternal life.

The secret was a plant at the bottom of the sea. Gilgamesh picked it, but a snake ate it, so he did not live for ever.

These pictures are based on the style used by Sumerians and Babylonians on their cylinder seals. 31

Royal graves of Anatolia

The people of Anatolia, which is the area now called Turkey, were among the world's first farmers. Later they acquired wealth through trading metal.

Anatolia was divided into several kingdoms, each with its own rulers. Rich royal graves have been found in some cities, dated between 2400BC and 2200BC.

This scene shows the king of Alaca Hüyük being buried. His favourite dog has been killed so that he can accompany his master on the last journey.

The royal tomb has been opened so that the king's body can be laid next to that of his queen, who died a number of years before.

Dorak
Troy
ANATOLIA
Alaca • Hüyük
Kültepe •
MEDITERRANEAN SEA

Cattle for slaughter

King

Cattle will be slaughtered and their heads placed on top of the grave, when it is closed.

Body of queen

The new kingdom

The period archaeologists call the New Kingdom of Egypt began about 1567BC. Egypt was already an old civilisation with great achievements, but now a new age began. Great warrior kings like Tuthmosis III, Amenhotep II, Seti I and Ramesses II won a great empire. It was a time of great wealth, mighty temple buildings and religious conflicts. Only one king's tomb escaped being robbed in ancient times – that of Tutankhamun. His treasures give us an idea of the fabulous riches that must once have been in Egypt.

Female Pharoah

Queen Hatshepsut, who was one of the few women pharoahs of Egypt, inspects her new temple building at Deir el Bahari. With her is her architect Senenmut. The temple still stands today, though much of the paint has worn off.

The paintings and hieroglyphs on the temple walls describe events in Queen Hatshepsut's life.

This is part of Abu Simbel, a mighty rock-cut temple in Nubia, which was built by Ramesses II.

Senenmut

Hatshepsut

The Egyptian Empire

By 1500BC, many countries in the Middle East already had long, interesting histories. Then, there was a great new burst of activity. Countries began to trade, win empires and set up colonies.

The Egyptians had lived peacefully since about 3120BC. The only province they had conquered in this time was Nubia, their neighbour in the south. Between 1670 and 1567BC, a people called the Hyksos crossed the eastern frontier and conquered Egypt.

The Egyptians built huge forts, like this one, on their frontiers. But the Hyksos had horses and chariots and they galloped past before the Egyptians could stop them.

The Hyksos ruled parts of Egypt for about 100 years before the Egyptians attacked them. Most Egyptian soldiers fought on foot, with spears, bows and arrows and no body armour.

The pharaoh's court

The pharaoh and his queen received ambassadors from their empire, who brought gifts and goods to trade. Here, Syrians and Nubians pay tribute to an Egyptian pharaoh.

The Egyptians had their own gold mines and could use gold to buy things they lacked, like timber. They imported silver, copper, horses, slaves, ivory and exotic African animals.

Lady courtiers

Gold

Syrians

Slave girl

Nubians

Pet baboon for the queen

Ivory

Pharaoh's wore a special war crown.

Egyptians learned to use horses and chariots to force the Hyksos out of Egypt. Then, they attacked neighbouring lands.

Reports of battles were written on temple walls. Within 70 years, Egyptians controlled the largest empire of their time.

This map shows the Egyptian empire in 1450BC. The Mitanni and the Hittites in the north were rivals of the Egyptians.

Trade with other lands

Cretans and later Mycenaeans, traded with Egyptians, bringing Cretan, Greek and other Mediterranean products to Egypt.

Egyptians visited a land they called Punt, which historians think was in East Africa. They bought incense there.

Sinai was the source of Egypt's turquoise. Donkey caravans took supplies to the mines and brought back the turquoise.

Travel in ancient Egypt

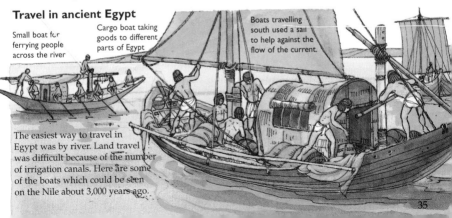

Small boat for ferrying people across the river

Cargo boat taking goods to different parts of Egypt

Boats travelling south used a sail to help against the flow of the current.

The easiest way to travel in Egypt was by river. Land travel was difficult because of the number of irrigation canals. Here are some of the boats which could be seen on the Nile about 3,000 years ago.

35

Houses and furniture

This is a city street in ancient Egypt. Models show that in cities, where land was scarce, the Egyptians built houses up to five storeys high.

In Egypt, only temples and tombs, which were built to stand for ever, were made of stone. All other buildings were made of sun-dried bricks. Rich people had their houses plastered and painted.

Very few Egyptian cities can be excavated because modern cities are built on top of the old ones. However, models and paintings from tombs show us what ancient Egyptian houses looked like in both town and country.

Bedroom

Head-rest

The Egyptians used stone or wooden head-rests on their beds instead of pillows. They kept their clothes in chests and their jewellery and cosmetics in small boxes.

People spent a lot of time on the roofs of their houses because it was cooler and they could enjoy the evening breeze. Sometimes they slept on the roof too.

Bathroom

Taking a shower

Rich people had bathrooms and lavatories in their houses. The bathroom walls were lined with stone to stop the splashes damaging the mud bricks.

Making bricks

1. The hard, dry earth was broken up with digging sticks and piled into baskets.

2. Water and chopped straw were trodden into the mud. The mixture was put in moulds.

3. The bricks were left to dry in the hot sun. It took several days for them to dry hard.

Furniture

Archaeologists have been able to find many pieces of actual furniture because the Egyptians buried furniture with the dead for use in the Next World. The greatest find was from the tomb of King Tutankhamun. The rich inlaid furniture shown here is of the type owned by noblemen.

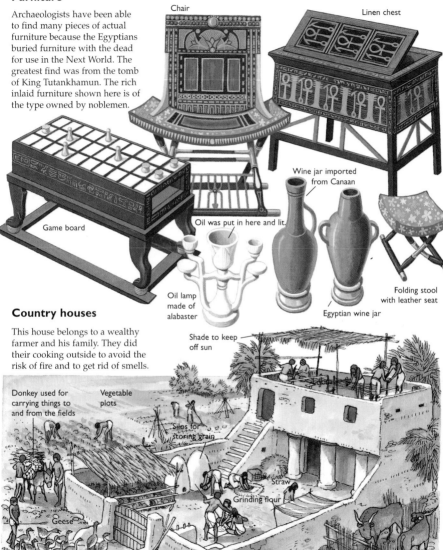

Chair

Linen chest

Game board

Wine jar imported from Canaan

Oil was put in here and lit.

Oil lamp made of alabaster

Egyptian wine jar

Folding stool with leather seat

Country houses

This house belongs to a wealthy farmer and his family. They did their cooking outside to avoid the risk of fire and to get rid of smells.

Shade to keep off sun

Donkey used for carrying things to and from the fields

Vegetable plots

Silos for storing grain

Straw

Grinding flour

Geese

Temples

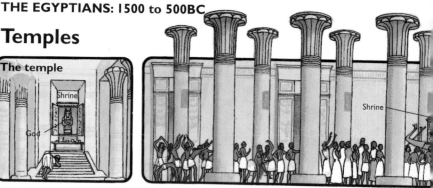

The temple

Shrine

God

Shrine

A statue of a god or goddess was kept in a shrine in every Egyptian temple. Each day, priests bathed, clothed and "fed" the statue, then prayed to it.

The main part of the temple was a huge columned hall. Its walls and pillars were covered with religious pictures and texts. Ordinary people were not allowed in here or in the inner sanctuary where the shrine was kept. They had to stay outside in the courtyard. On festival days, they could see the shrine containing the god.

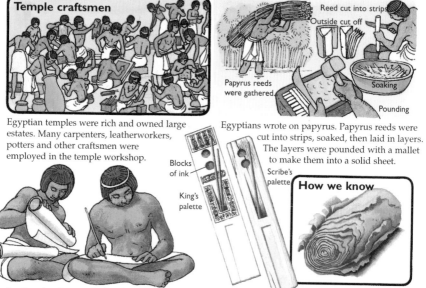

Temple craftsmen

Egyptian temples were rich and owned large estates. Many carpenters, leatherworkers, potters and other craftsmen were employed in the temple workshop.

Papyrus reeds were gathered.

Reed cut into strips

Outside cut off

Soaking

Pounding

Egyptians wrote on papyrus. Papyrus reeds were cut into strips, soaked, then laid in layers. The layers were pounded with a mallet to make them into a solid sheet.

Blocks of ink

King's palette

Scribe's palette

How we know

Armies of scribes worked in the temples. Many spent their time copying texts onto rolls of papyrus. They wrote in picture signs, called hieroglyphs.

The scribes wrote with brushes. Their ink was made in solid blocks and had to be used with water. Brushes and inks were kept in palettes, like these.

Only a few papyrus rolls have survived and these are badly damaged. Scholars are able to learn a great deal about life in ancient Egypt from them.

Gods

Osiris

Horus

Anubis

Thoth

Hathor

Isis

Taweret

Amen-Re

Apis

Ptah

Sekhmet

Priests lifted the shrine on to a model boat, then carried it around the city, accompanied by temple dancers and musicians.

The picture above shows some of the Egyptians' gods and goddesses. They were often painted or carved in the shape of animals, or at least with animals' heads. This was so that they could be easily recognised, even by people who could not read. Amen-Re was the chief of the gods.

Mathematics

The Egyptians were excellent mathematicians. Some of their texts show how they planned buildings calculating the men and materials needed.

Medicine

Surviving medical texts show the Egyptians were skilled doctors. These texts give details of treatments, medicines, prayers and spells.

Telling the time

Position of water level shows what time it is

Water drips out of here.

This water clock was an Egyptian invention to tell the time. Egyptians also worked out the 365 day calendar by studying the stars and planets.

Make a water clock

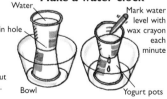

Water

Mark water level with wax crayon each minute

Pin hole

Bowl

Yogurt pots

Fill up the top pot with water. Mark the water level with a wax crayon. Using a clock or watch, mark the water level each minute. Then fill the pot to use the clock.

Key dates

1570	**Ahmosis I** drove out the Hyksos. Beginning of empire.
1525/1512	**Tuthmosis I.** Warrior pharaoh who reached the River Euphrates on a raid. First King to have a rock-cut tomb in the Valley of the Kings at Thebes.
1503/1482	**Hatshepsut.** Queen who became pharaoh.
1504/1450	**Tuthmosis III.** Hatshepsut's stepson. She kept him from power when he was young, but he later became the greatest of Egypt's warrior pharaohs.
1378/1362	**Akhenaten.** Pharaoh who tried to persuade Egyptians there was only one god. He was married to Nefertiti.
1361/1352	**Tutankhamun.** Boy pharaoh whose magnificent treasure was found by archaeologist Howard Carter in AD 1922.
1304/1237	**Ramesses II**, also called **Ramesses the Great.** Warrior pharaoh who fought the Hittites in the Battle of Kadesh.
1198/1166	**Ramesses III.** The last of the great warrior pharaohs. He saved Egypt from the Sea Peoples.
1166	After the death of Ramesses III, the power of Egypt slowly declined and the empire was lost.
751/671	Nubians ruled Egypt.
671/664	Assyrians ruled Egypt.
525/404	Persians ruled Egypt.
332	**Alexander the Great** conquered Egypt.

Approximate BC dates

39

Warriors of Anatolia

The Hittites were a tough warrior people. No-one is certain where they came from, but around 2000BC they arrived in Anatolia, which is in modern Turkey. The people they found there lived in rich cities, each ruled by its own king. By 1680BC, the Hittites had defeated them all. About 200 years later, the Hittites began conquering the lands around them and built up an empire.

ANATOLIA

• Hattusas

• Kültepe

MEDITERRANEAN SEA

Kiln for baking clay tablets

Donkeys carrying copper ore

Part of this wall has been removed so you can see inside.

Firewood for kiln

Copper was found in Anatolia. Assyrian copper merchants built this trading post there in about 2000BC.

The Hittites later forced out foreign traders and took over the metal trade themselves. This made them very powerful because everyone needed metal for tools and weapons.

About 1500BC, the Hittites began trading iron which is much stronger than copper. This dagger has an iron blade. It was probably a gift from the Hittites to Tutankhamun.

Key dates

2000	Hittites arrive in Anatolia.
1680/1650	**King Labarnas I** united the land.
1460	Beginning of Hittite empire.
1380/1340	**King Shuppiluliuma** extended empire into Syria and broke power of Mitanni.
1300	Battle of Kadesh against Ramesses II of Egypt.
1283	Peace treaty with Ramesses II.
1270	Hittite princess married Ramesses II.
1190	Hittites defeated by Sea Peoples. End of kingdom in Anatolia. Small states survive in Syria.
700	These states disappear in Assyrian empire.

Approximate BC dates

Hittite gods

Carvings are here

This gorge was sacred to the Hittites. They carved pictures of their gods and goddesses into the rock-face. In front of the gorge are the ruins of a temple.

Teshub

This picture shows some of the gods and goddesses which are carved in the sacred gorge. The chief god was Teshub, who was thought to control the weather.

40

Hittite cities

The Hittites built massive defences with huge blocks of stone to guard their cities and palaces. This is part of the wall which surrounded their capital city, Hattusas.

Gateway to city

Hittite warriors

Secret passage

The Hittites dug narrow tunnels under their city walls. During a siege, they would dash out and surprise the enemy.

The Hittites' horses were too small to carry riders far. Warriors rode into battle in chariots pulled by two or more horses.

Hittite warriors destroyed the Mitanni people and took their land. They also captured part of the Egyptians' empire.

Peace treaty

After years of war, the Hittites made peace with the Egyptians. In 1270BC a Hittite princess married the Egyptian king, Ramesses II. They signed a treaty – the first international treaty between two countries.

The end of the Hittites

About 1200BC, the Hittite empire was wiped out by new invaders called the Sea Peoples, who probably came from the Mediterranean islands. They brought their families with them to look for new homes.

Some Hittite refugees escaped to the south and settled in what is now called Syria. They managed to survive there until the area was conquered by the Assyrians, 500 years later.

Mysterious people from Greece

The Mycenaeans are named after the city of Mycenae in Greece where their remains were first discovered in AD1876. Historians disagree about who they were, but some think they were newcomers to the area, related to the people who began arriving all over the Middle East around 2000BC.

This is the gold funeral mask of one of the first kings of Mycenae. It was thought to be a portrait of Agamemnon, who led a famous war against Troy, but it is now known to be earlier.

Mycenae was found by a German archaeologist called Schliemann. One of his greatest discoveries was this circle of royal graves dated between 1600 and 1500BC.

We have removed part of the mound of earth so you can see inside.

Tombs of the warrior kings

After 1500BC, the warrior kings of Mycenae and the other city-states in Greece were buried in tombs like this, called tholos tombs.

Doorway

This tomb, found at Mycenae, was called the Treasury of Atreus, because it was thought at first that it belonged to Agamemnon's father, Atreus.

The king's body, with his weapons and treasures, was placed in this beehive-shaped stone vault. The treasure was stolen from this tomb in ancient times and it was found empty.

The Mycenaean warrior kings became rich and powerful and eventually rivalled the Cretans. When Crete was destroyed, they took control of the seas.

Key dates

2200/2000	New people arrived in Greece.
1600/1500	Grave circles at Mycenae. Mycenaeans influenced by Crete.
1450	Mycenaeans appear to have taken over Knossos in Crete. Linear B tablets in Crete as well as in Greece.
1400	Mycenaeans were great sea power. They traded widely.
1200	Siege of Troy. Slow decline of Mycenaean power.
1100/800	Dark Age in Greece.

Approximate BC dates

These are some of the objects found in the royal graves. Some of them, especially the bull's head, show that the Mycenaeans were influenced by the Cretans.

This tablet lists horses and chariots.

The Mycenaeans' language was an early form of Greek. It was written in a script we call Linear B. Many tablets have been found, but they are only lists of stored goods, showing that barley, wine and olive oil produced by local farmers were stored in the palace. They tell us nothing of the Mycenaeans' history or their thoughts.

This Mycenaean gold ring shows a goddess attended by her priestesses. As in Crete, goddesses and priestesses were very powerful, though tablets name some gods, too.

Mycenaean treasure

A balloon full of air is tied to the ingot to lift it to the surface.

"Ox-hide" ingot

Underwater archaeologists have rescued cargo from the wrecks of Mycenaean ships. The Mycenaeans sailed great distances to trade metals and other goods. They carried copper ingots shaped like stretched-out ox hides, like the one shown here.

How we know

Mycenaeans traded valuable objects made by craftsmen for things they needed from abroad. The presence of their special style of pottery, silver and gold work in other countries shows how far they travelled.

Silver bowl

Gold earrings

Pottery vase

Perfume jar

Carved ivory of two women and a child, which shows us the clothes they wore.

Palaces and soldiers

Mycenaean kings lived in great palaces. A porch and a reception room led into the megaron, which was a central hall, like this one, with a throne. The walls were covered with bright frescoes, which are pictures painted while the plaster was still damp.

There were many other rooms in the palace, including stores and record offices. Bedrooms were upstairs.

Bards sang songs in praise of the king.

Bronze helmet covered with boars' tusks.

Bronze armour

Perfume jar

Bath made of stone

Step

Shield covered with animal skin

A bath like the one in this picture, was found in the palace at Pylos. Walled cities like Pylos, Mycenae and Athens had secret passages to underground springs, so they had water even during a siege.

We know about armour and weapons because weapons were found in graves, and pictures of soldiers have survived. It was probably only very noble or successful warriors who had complete suits of armour and boars' tusk helmets.

Hunting wild boars

Important warriors owned horses and chariots. When they were not at war they used them for hunting. The helmets they wore in battle were often decorated with tusks of wild boars killed in the hunt.

The Lion Gate

Many palaces and cities were protected by massive stone walls. This is the Lion Gate in the wall around Mycenae as it stands today.

The Trojan wars

This engraving on silver shows the siege of a city. A famous Greek story tells how the Mycenaeans sailed east to the city of Troy and laid a siege to it for ten years.

Wars between the Mycenaean kingdoms may have weakened them, because about 1100BC, new people, called the Dorians invaded some areas of Greece. The power of the Mycenaeans declined, though their glory lived on in the poems of the Greek poet Homer.

Rich Mycenaean ladies wore dresses like this. Helen of Troy, a beautiful lady who was supposed to have been the cause of the wars with Troy, would have dressed like this too.

Canaanites and Philistines

The people who settled at the eastern end of the Mediterranean about 2000BC are called Canaanites. Their land was rich and it also formed an important link between Asia and Africa. Rival empire builders such as the Egyptians, Mitanni and Hittites constantly fought over it.

By 1500BC there were many walled city-states in Canaan. They were heavily defended. Each had a royal family and palace. This statue is of a Canaanite prince.

This piece of ivory shows a Canaanite prince being welcomed home after a battle. The princes were always fighting each other instead of keeping out invaders.

Huge cedar trees grew in Canaan. Mesopotamians and Egyptians wanted these as they had no good wood of their own. This is why they wanted to gain control of the area.

The port of Byblos

Merchant

Scribe

Slaves

Engraved gold trays

Wine jars

Cedar wood

Canaanite craftsmen were very skilled. They made beautiful objects from gold and ivory which were sold to other countries. In this picture, a Canaanite merchant is

preparing to set out from the great port of Byblos in about 1450BC. He is going to take slaves, wood, wine, gold and ivory to his best customers, the Egyptians.

Canaanite gods

Canaanite script

Clay tablets, like this, were found in the remains of the city of Ugarit. They are covered with Canaanite writing which tells of the adventures of gods and godesses.

Two of the gods are shown here. Canaanites believed their gods controlled the weather and made crops grow. They worshipped them in "High Places" which had tall stones inside.

The Sea Peoples invade

About 1190BC, the Sea Peoples invaded the eastern Mediterranean, killing and destroying as they went. Here they are fighting the Egyptians, who finally defeated them.

One tribe of Sea Peoples, the Peleset retreated to the south of Canaan and settled there. This land was named Palestine after them and in the Bible, they are called Philistines.

Philistines

Egyptians

Philistines controlled the iron trade. Iron weapons are stronger than other metals, so the Philistines were feared.

47

Nomads in the desert

Our earliest records show that tribes wandered along the edges of the Arabian and Syrian deserts with their sheep. Such people are called nomads.

This is part of an Egyptian tomb painting of about 1900BC. It shows the arrival of nomad traders who have brought eye-paint to sell in Egypt. They carry all their belongings on the backs of donkeys. Other tribes owned sheep and goats which they took to the Delta of Egypt to eat grass.

In some places nomads were able to settle among farmers. If too many arrived, the locals drove them away.

This statue is of a king, about 2000BC, whose tribe invaded and became the rulers of Mari, a city in Mesopotamia.

Solomon's temple

This temple was built in Jerusalem by the Israelite king, Solomon. Solomon and his father, David, were friendly with the Phoenician king, Hiram, of Tyre. Hiram sent skilled Phoenician craftsmen to Jerusalem to help design and build the temple. It is very similar in plan to earlier temples built by the Canaanites.

Wood carvings covered with gold leaf

Cedar wood beams

Altar

Some nomads, like the girl musician here, hired themselves out as servants.

By about 1000BC, people had learnt to tame camels. This meant they could cross the desert.

The Israelites

Among the wandering tribes were the ancestors of the Israelites. After many battles, they took some land from the Canaanites and settled down.

The Philistines were rivals. The Israelites chose Saul as king to lead them against the Philistines. The hero of the war is said to have been a boy called David.

David became king in about 1010BC and made Jerusalem his capital. This great bronze bowl stood outside the temple built there by his son Solomon.

Under King Solomon, the Israelites traded widely and grew rich. After Solomon died in 925BC, the kingdom split in two – Judah and Israel.

The Assyrians extended their empire towards Israel. This monument shows King Jehu of Israel paying tribute to them. Later, Israel rebelled. Its people were taken away, never to return.

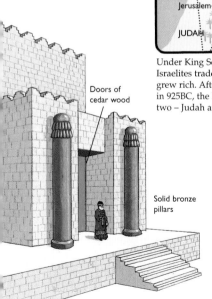

Doors of cedar wood

Solid bronze pillars

The people of Judah escaped the Assyrians, but were conquered by the Babylonians in 587BC. Jerusalem and the temple were destroyed.

Many of these people and places are mentioned in the Old Testament of the Bible. 49

The Phoenicians

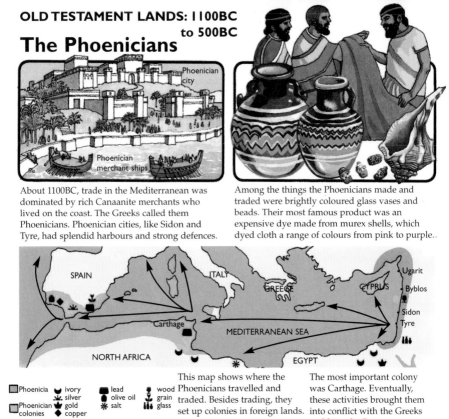

Phoenician city

Phoenician merchant ships

About 1100BC, trade in the Mediterranean was dominated by rich Canaanite merchants who lived on the coast. The Greeks called them Phoenicians. Phoenician cities, like Sidon and Tyre, had splendid harbours and strong defences.

Among the things the Phoenicians made and traded were brightly coloured glass vases and beads. Their most famous product was an expensive dye made from murex shells, which dyed cloth a range of colours from pink to purple.

SPAIN · **ITALY** · **GREECE** · **CYPRUS** · Ugarit · Byblos · Sidon · Tyre · Carthage · **MEDITERRANEAN SEA** · **NORTH AFRICA** · **EGYPT**

☐ Phoenicia   ♥ ivory   ■ lead   ♠ wood
♣ silver   ● olive oil   ♠ grain
☐ Phoenician   ♥ gold   ✳ salt   ♣♣♣ glass
colonies   ◆ copper

This map shows where the Phoenicians travelled and traded. Besides trading, they set up colonies in foreign lands.

The most important colony was Carthage. Eventually, these activities brought them into conflict with the Greeks and later the Romans.

Carthage

Pottery urns

The Phoenician princess Dido founded Carthage. When she landed on the north African coast, she asked the local ruler for land to build a city on.

He said she could have as much land as an ox-hide would cover. Dido had the hide cut into very thin strips so she could mark off a large area of land.

Occasionally in times of great trouble, Phoenicians sacrificed children to their gods. The burnt remains were placed in pottery urns and buried.

Phoenicians and Israelites were on good terms. Ahab, king of Israel, married Jezebel, princess of Tyre. Phoenician craftsmen helped build Solomon's temple.

The Phoenicians were skilled sailors and daring explorers. One expedition visited the west coast of Africa and another sailed right round it.

Part of the Phoenician alphabet

ВＹ∠ＶＹφ
ＨＫＬＭＮＱ

Letters in our alphabet which have come from the Phoenician ones.

Perhaps the greatest of all the Phoenicians' achievements was the invention of their alphabet, which is the basis of the alphabet we use today.

War ships

The Phoenicians were famous for their war ships.

This warship is a bireme, which means it has two banks of oars.

Key dates

1100	Rise to power of Phoenicians.
970/936	**Hiram the Great**, king of Tyre.
876	Tyre paid tribute to Assyria.
875	**Jezebel** married Ahab of Israel.
814	**Dido** founded Carthage.
600	Phoenicians sailed round Africa.
574	Tyre defeated by Babylon.
539	Phoenicia became part of Persian empire with fall of Babylon.
	Approximate BC dates

Later Phoenicia became part of the Persian empire. The Persians used Phoenician war ships to fight great sea battles against the Greeks.

Ram for making holes in enemy ships

51

Life in the Assyrian Empire

In early times, Assyria was a small, unimportant state in northern Mesopotamia. For centuries it was ruled by more powerful states, such as Akkad and Babylon. When these collapsed, the Assyrians had the chance to become independent and win an empire of their own.

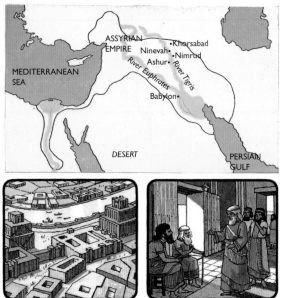

This carving shows one of the Assyrians' gods. Their chief god was Ashur. They also had a mother goddess, Ishtar, and believed in demons and spirits.

This is the capital city of Assyria, named Ashur after the god. It was built on the River Tigris so that trading ships could unload there.

Ashur had a powerful Council of Elders which was often in conflict with the king. Many kings tried to reduce its power.

The Assyrians had a code of laws. People who broke them were punished savagely. Some were flogged or had their ears cut off.

This is an Assyrian library. The language and literature inherited from Sumer and Babylon were stored on tablets made of clay.

The Assyrians dug deep wells in the ground, in their cities so that if the city was besieged, the people would still have water.

The empire

Ashurnasirpal II

1. For centuries, the Assyrian peasants had to fight for survival. They became good, tough warriors.

2. Ashurnasirpal II's grandfather, Adadnirari II, made Assyria independent and an empire.

3. By 670BC the empire was too big to be controlled properly. First Egypt, then Babylon, broke away.

4. By 609BC, the empire was destroyed. Its ruins lay in the desert until they were discovered in the 1840s.

Watering the land

This is a shaduf. The Assyrians used shadufs to lift river water into canals dug specially to take it to the fields.

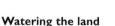
Stone weight

When the land was watered properly, it was fertile. The Assyrians grew wheat, barley, grapes, fruit trees and vegetables.

This aqueduct was built to take water to Ninevah so that King Sennacherib could have gardens and orchards planted there.

Make a model shaduf
Use this model shaduf to lift water

Scissors

Bag

3. Hole

Bottle top

1. Tie on string

2. Tie to stick

4. Paper clip

5. Plasticine® weight

Bottle

1. Tie string onto corner cut from plastic bag. 2. Tie onto stick. 3. Cut hole in bottle top. 4. Push in paper clip. 5. Screw lid on bottle. Add Plasticine® weight.

The weight at the end of the pole balanced the bucket when it was full. The farmer then swung the pole around and emptied the bucket into the canal.

Kings and their palaces

The palaces were decorated inside with glazed tiles and stone carvings showing the king's great deeds.

The Assyrians believed that their land belonged to the god Ashur. The king, as Ashur's servant, ruled the land, waged war in his name, built temples, appointed priests and led important religious festivals.

Assyrian kings usually had many wives and children. The son, chosen by the king to be his heir was specially educated in the "House of the Succession" to be a good ruler.

This is King Ashurnasirpal II in the throne room of his palace. The king received royal messengers from all parts of the empire who kept him in touch with what was happening.

Ashurnasirpal II and several other kings fought to enlarge the empire. To celebrate, they used prisoners of war to build cities and splendid palaces in Nimrud, Khorsabad and Ninevah.

King's personal servant

Servant carrying the king's weapon

The palace garden

This scene shows King Ashurbanipal in his garden with the queen, his servants and musicians.

The garden is planted with exotic trees and flowers from all over the empire.

Musicians

Lion hunting

When not leading the army in war, the king hunted to show his skill and bravery. Lions were brought specially to his hunting parks.

Lions were kept in cages until the king was ready for them.

Walls of soldiers with their shields stop the lions escaping.

King Ashurbanipal

Grape vines

Queen

Servants with fans

Furniture decorated with gold and ivory inlays

The Assyrian army

Going to battle

The Assyrians had to fight continually to keep their empire under control. This army is setting out to attack a city which has rebelled against their ruler.

The foot soldiers were armed with bows and arrows, slings for hurling stones, or lances. The cavalry, that is the soldiers on horseback, also used bows and lances.

Horse-drawn chariots each carried a team of driver, bowman and shield-bearer. The army also had siege engines which had battering rams and space inside for bowmen.

Ransacking the captured city

Often, the Assyrians completely destroyed the captured city and the farmland around it. They took its treasure as booty and either killed the citizens or took them captive.

Soldiers knock down the city walls.

Houses in the city have been set on fire.

Orchards are burnt.

Valuable goods and animals are taken away as booty.

Heads of dead citizens are collected and counted.

Captives are led away.

Some of the captives became slaves, but others were sent to live in new cities. The Assyrians hoped their experiences would teach them not to rebel again.

Soldiers swam across rivers clutching inflated animal skins to keep afloat. The horses swam too. The chariots were rowed across in small round boats.

Holes for firing arrows through.

Inside a siege engine

The siege engines were made of wood and covered with animal's skins. They could be pushed up to the city walls with several bowmen hidden inside. The ram was used for breaking down gates and undermining walls.

The engine was moved by soldiers pushing from behind.

The battering ram was raised and lowered by this rope.

Wooden frame   Animal skins

When they reached the city, heavily armed soldiers scaled the walls with ladders while bowmen and slingers fired from further away. Siege engines battered the wall and gate.

Key dates

2000	**Pazur-Ashur I** reigned about the time Assyria became independent of Sumerian empire.
1814/1782	**Shamsi-Adad I.** First king to extend Assyria's frontiers.
911/891	**Adad-nirari II** united his people.
883/859	**Ashurnasirpal II**
858/824	**Sargon II**
704/681	**Sennacherib**
668/631	**Ashurbanipal**
614/609	Complete destruction of empire.

Approximate BC dates

Local prince
Assyrian official
Conspirators planning rebellion

Some conquered lands, such as Egypt, were ruled by local princes, but Assyrian officials stayed to make sure they were loyal. Even so, as the empire grew, rebellions were common.

People bringing tribute
Assyrian scribe

Conquered people had to pay tribute to the Assyrians. Failure to do so was rapidly punished and the Assyrians were notorious for the cruel tortures they inflicted on people.

The City of Babylon

The ancient city of Babylon stood on the banks of the River Euphrates. Under its king, Hammurabi, Babylon controlled an empire, but this gradually broke up after he died about 1750BC.

Babylon was then ruled peacefully by a people called the Kassites. In 1171BC, the Kassites were driven out by the Elamites. The Assyrians then claimed to rule Babylon, but some Babylonians resisted them.

The marshes of southern Mesopotamia made a good hiding place for Babylonians fighting against Assyrian rule. One of their leaders was Merodach-Baladan.

The Babylonians defeated the Assyrians in 612BC, with the help of their neighbours, the Medes. Nebuchadnezzar, the son of their general, went on to win an empire.

Telling the future

The Babylonians believed they could tell the future by looking at a sheep's liver. This clay model shows the parts for the priests to look at.

Key dates

Approximate BC dates

Ishtar Gate

Processional way

Part of the New Year procession

The city of Babylon was rebuilt by Nebuchadnezzar. It became one of the richest cities in the world. The gateway, called the Ishtar Gate was covered with glazed blue tiles. Nearby was Nebuchadnezzar's palace, with its famous Hanging Garden.

This huge ziggurat and temple, which Nebuchadnezzar built, was dedicated to the Babylonians' chief god, Marduk.

Nebuchadnezzar's palace

Water from the river was used to water the Hanging Gardens.

These are the Hanging Gardens of Babylon. They were built by Nebuchadnezzar for his wife Amytis, a princess of the Medes, because she missed the hilly landscape of her home.

Processional Way

The people of Babylon are watching a procession make its way to the temple of Marduk for the New Year festival. Old traditions like this were revived when Babylon was rebuilt.

City walls

The goddess Ishtar

This is a statue of Ishtar, the chief goddess of Babylon, after whom the great gate was named. It is carved from alabaster and has rubies inlaid in it.

The end of Babylon

Royal Persian guardsmen

In 539BC, Babylon was taken over by the Persians whose power was rapidly increasing. People gradually left the city. By AD200, it was deserted and ruined.

Monument Builders

The climate of North Europe is so damp that things buried in the ground decay quickly and leave little trace for archaeologists. Because of this we know less about the people of Europe than about the people of the Middle East. No texts have been found, so we do not know if they could write. From very early times, people in Europe built great stone monuments. The treasures that have survived show they were highly skilled craftsmen.

After about 600BC, some Celts spread out across Europe in these directions.

Treasures of Europe

These pictures show just a few examples of the fine craftsmanship of the people who lived in Europe in ancient times.

Rock carvings like this were found in Sweden and Norway. They often show ships carrying the Sun across the sky.

This bronze helmet is from Vixo in Denmark. It was probably not worn in battle because it is too heavy and awkward.

This is a bronze model of a chariot carrying the Sun. It was thrown into a marsh in Denmark as an offering to the gods.

Metalworkers in Europe were very skilled. This helmet and armour came from Villanova in Italy.

This enormous bronze wine jar was made in Greece and then taken to France. It was buried in the grave of a princess.

Building Stonehenge

The most impressive ancient stone circle is Stonehenge in southern England. Work began on it about 2750BC. It was changed several times. This scene shows the last and most impressive version being built. It was finished soon after 1500BC.

Stone pounders make hollows in lintels.

About a thousand men are needed to pull one of the sarsen stones from the quarry over 32km away.

This is Stonehenge completed. It was probably a temple but some scholars think it was also used as a calendar.

Lintel

Bluestones

Sarsen

These "bluestones" were brought from Wales and were used in an earlier stone circle. When this stone circle is finished, they will be put in the middle of it.

Wooden rollers are placed under the sledge to make it move more easily.

Sarsen being raised into position in its hole.

These lumps fit in hollows on lintels.

Sledge

The upright stones are called sarsens.

The chalky earth is taken away in baskets.

Tree-trunk lever

Pick made of antler

These men are digging a hole for the next sarsen.

The lintels are lifted up on towers of logs placed criss-cross. The layers of logs are slipped under the stone one at a time to gradually raise the lintel to the top of the sarsens.

61

First civilisation in China

Civilisation in China began near the Yellow River. Shang kings ruled for about 500 years, until they were conquered by the Chou in 1057BC.

The first farmers of northern China grew millet and kept cattle and pigs. They probably lived in pit houses dug out of the ground.

The kings lived in palaces built of wood and earth.

Pit houses with thatched roofs

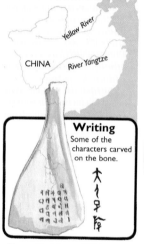

Writing

Some of the characters carved on the bone.

The earliest form of Chinese writing is found cut into animal bones. These were used for taking messages, thought to come from the gods.

A Chou noble drives away from the king's palace in his war chariot. The chariot had no seat, just a platform to stand on.

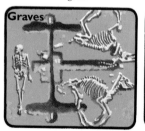

Graves

Chinese archaeologists opened the tombs of the Shang kings near Anyang. They found the skeletons of horses and charioteers with their chariots.

Bronze vessel

The Shang king thought his ancestors were gods. He offered them meat and wine in bronze vessels. Many Chinese still honour their ancestors today.

Jade ornaments like this animal were sewn to the dead person's clothes. Objects like this dagger were put in graves of nobles and rich people.

First farmers in America

Many different tribes lived in Central and Southern America. It seems that they became farmers later than the people in the Middle East.

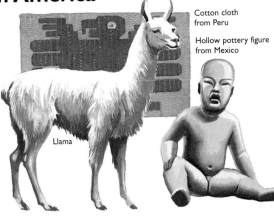

Cotton cloth from Peru

Hollow pottery figure from Mexico

Llama

NORTH AMERICA

MEXICO

PERU

SOUTH AMERICA

Olmec carving made of jade

Farmers had grown cotton since 3000BC. They spun and wove it by hand to make cloth with designs like the one above. They got wool from llamas and alpacas.

Their most important crop was maize, which first appeared in Mexico in 2500BC. Pottery, like this figure, was being made from 2300BC onwards.

The Olmecs

The Olmecs, first of the famous cultures of this area, appear about 1200BC. You can recognize their statues and jade and pottery figures by their "baby" faces.

In Mexico, the Olmecs were building shrines on great mounds by 600BC. At this time they had no wheels or metal tools, so the buildings were an amazing achievement.

India

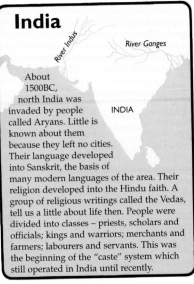

River Indus

River Ganges

INDIA

About 1500BC, north India was invaded by people called Aryans. Little is known about them because they left no cities. Their language developed into Sanskrit, the basis of many modern languages of the area. Their religion developed into the Hindu faith. A group of religious writings called the Vedas, tell us a little about life then. People were divided into classes – priests, scholars and officials; kings and warriors; merchants and farmers; labourers and servants. This was the beginning of the "caste" system which still operated in India until recently.

The Dark Ages

The years 1100BC to 700BC in Greece are called the Dark Ages as so little is known about them. New people called the Dorians invaded and after that no more great palaces were built. People lived simply. They burnt their dead instead of burying them with offerings.

It became easier to get iron, so people could make strong tools and weapons. Greece was divided into several city-states, such as Corinth, Athens and Sparta, which often quarrelled amongst themselves.

As the numbers of people grew, many went abroad. Some set up colonies in other countries and traded. Others hired themselves out to foreign kings as soldiers.

The Greeks were the first people to make coins of a standard weight and quality of metal. These made trade much easier and the traders became very rich.

By trading and setting up colonies around the Mediterranean, the Greeks grew prosperous. They became dangerous competitors for the Phoenician merchants.

Homer

Homer composed poems about the siege of Troy and the adventures of a hero called Odysseus. His poems were passed on by word of mouth until writing came into use again.

Greek letters
ABEKMNRT
Our letters
ABEKMNRT

The Greeks took over the Phoenician alphabet and adapted it to suit their own needs. It was so simple to use that many people could learn to read and write.

Soldiers

This picture shows Greek soldiers called Hoplites. They fought in closely packed ranks, each man protecting the one next to him with his shield.

Iron spears

In cities, people rebelled against the unjust ruling nobles and helped new leaders seize power. These people were known as "tyrants".

Conquerors

The land we now call Iran was invaded by new people about 1200BC. The invaders seem to have come from somewhere in Europe, like many others who arrived in the Middle East, from 2000BC onwards.

One Iranian tribe, called the Medes, became powerful and in 612BC helped to destroy the empire of the Assyrians. Another group were the Persians, who later took over the Babylonian empire. Led by a great king called Cyrus, the Persians then won a huge empire of their own.

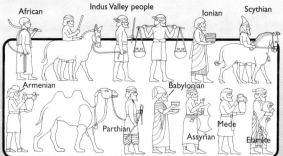

The palace of Persepolis was burned down in 330BC by Alexander the Great, but some of the carvings survived. These pictures are of carvings on one of the great staircases. They show some of the people conquered by the Persians. They are bringing horses, camels, skins, cloth and gold as tribute to the Persian king.

Persepolis

King Darius, a successor of Cyrus, began building an enormous palace at Persepolis in 518BC. The great hall, shown here, was big enough to hold 10,000 people.

Great Hall

Visitors were led through many halls and terraces which were decorated with stone carvings. The palace does not seem to have been lived in by the kings. It was probably used for special ceremonies like the celebration of the New Year.

Important Persians and Medes wait to be received by the king.

65

The Persian Empire

The great Persian king, Darius I, ran his empire cleverly and efficiently. He collected taxes from all the conquered people, but allowed them to keep their own customs, religions and way of life, as long as they were obedient.

Darius appointed local governors, called satraps, to rule the provinces of the empire and used Persian soldiers to check that the satraps did not become too powerful.

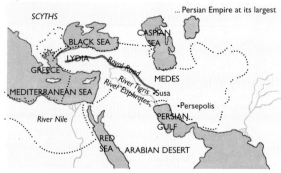

... Persian Empire at its largest

SCYTHS
BLACK SEA
CASPIAN SEA
LYDIA
Royal Road
GREECE
River Tigris
MEDES
River Euphrates
Susa
MEDITERRANEAN SEA
Persepolis
River Nile
PERSIAN GULF
RED SEA
ARABIAN DESERT

King Darius I

Incense burners

The Persians lived in the land we now call Iran. They won a huge empire under their great king, Cyrus, whose successor, King Darius I, is shown here.

Darius organised the empire very efficiently. He appointed local governors, called satraps, to rule each province and used Persian soldiers to check that they did not become too powerful. He also built good roads so that messengers could travel quickly with news from all over the empire.

As long as conquered people paid their taxes, the Persians respected their customs. Here, officials check tax payments before sorting them.

Religion

Altar

Fire was sacred to Persians.

The Magi (priests) always kept a fire burning. Zarathushtra, a prophet, changed religion from the worship of many gods to that of one, Ahuramazda.

Key dates

2000/1800	The Aryans migrated from southern Russia.
628	Birth of **Zarathushtra**
559/529	Reign of **Cyrus the Great.**
547	**Cyrus** defeated King Croesus of Lydia.
521/486	Reign of **Darius I.**
513/512	First Asian invasion of Europe. Persians conquered Thrace and Macedon.
490	Persians defeated by Greeks at Battle of Marathon.
486/465	Reign of **Xerxes I**, son of Darius.
480	Persians defeated by Greeks at Salamis.
330	**Alexander** destroyed Persian Empire. Persepolis was burned.

Approximate BC dates

THE GREEKS: 500BC to 400BC

The Greeks at War

Until 1100BC, the Mycenaeans ruled Greece. Then the Dorians invaded and a troubled time followed. We call this the Greek Dark Ages. Prosperity gradually returned.

Meanwhile, the Persian empire was growing rapidly. The Persians conquered Lydia, until then a Greek area, ruled by King Croesus. Later, several of these cities, led by Athens, rebelled and the so-called "Persian Wars" began.

The Persian king, Darius I, invaded Greece, but was defeated at Marathon. The news was carried over 40km to Sparta by a runner. Our marathon race is named after this.

Darius' son, Xerxes continued the war with Greece. He built a bridge of boats, made by his Egyptian and Phoenician subjects, to get his army across the Hellespont.

The Athenians discovered a rich vein of silver in their mines and so had money to build a new fleet. They finally defeated the Persians in a battle off the coast of Salamis.

New buildings in Athens

Spartan soldiers

Athens became the greatest city of Greece and led a league of other Greek cities. Athens' new leader Pericles collected money from all the cities in the league, in case of further attacks from the Persians. He used this money to build fine buildings to replace those damaged in the Persian wars. This angered the other cities.

The state of Sparta led Athens' enemies in a terrible war, known as the Peloponnesian War. It lasted 27 years until Athens was defeated in 404BC.

Life in Athens

Town life almost disappeared in Greece during the Dark Ages, but as trade slowly increased, the cities grew again. A city and the land around it formed a city-state. The largest and most famous of these was Athens. It had a high place, called the Acropolis, where the people could go in times of danger. All the "citizens", that is all the free men, not women or slaves, took part in the running of the city by voting on important matters. This is called democracy and it was first used in Athens.

The Parthenon temple, built by Pericles for the goddess Athena.

The old city, called the Acropolis

The Sacred Way leads to the Acropolis.

The Agora where people met to argue about politics and buy and sell things.

Open-air restaurant

Grape vines

Trade with Athens

Piraeus, the port of Athens, is about 6km away. Goods from the Mediterranean were landed there, including grain from the Black Sea ports.

Theatre

Actors

Altar

Chorus

Orchestra

Padded actor from wall painting

Pottery copy of mask

A Greek theatre had a round area called the orchestra where the actors performed. The audience brought cushions because the seats were stone.

The idea of the theatre grew from dances at festivals to honour the gods. Later, writers like Euripedes and Sophocles produced plays for the theatre.

All the parts in plays were taken by men who wore masks and padding. Copies of masks were made to decorate buildings.

Politics

Discs meaning "guilty"

Disc meaning "not guilty"

Ostraka

Politician's name

All citizens discussed and voted on city matters. Our word "politics" comes from the Greek politikos, meaning "of the city".

There were no lawyers, so people had to present their own cases in court. Jurors showed verdicts with small discs like these.

A politician could be sent into exile if 6,000 citizens wrote his name on pieces of broken pottery like these, called ostraka.

The philosopher, Socrates was condemned because people feared the way he questioned everything. He chose to die and drank poison.

Pottery

Athens was famous for its pottery. Everyday things, like this baby's bottle and toy, were made of pottery, as well as vases painted with scenes of gods and heroes of daily life.

Potters' workshop

Potters' quarter of city

How we know

The scenes painted on vases tell us about Greek life. This one shows a boy buying sandals. He puts his foot on the leather as the shoemaker cuts round it.

These women are celebrating the festival of the god Dionysus. Most of the time women stayed at home and did not take part in public life.

Boys were well educated from the age of seven. This boy is learning to read. Music and sport were taught too. Girls were taught by their mothers at home.

THE GREEKS: 330BC to 140BC
Alexander the Great

The Greek city-states quarrelled among themselves even when the Peloponnesian War was over. Peace was not restored until Philip, King of Macedon took control. The Greeks thought him a barbarian. To them, this was anyone who was not Greek. Philip wanted to fight the Persians with Greek help, but died leaving his son, Alexander, to carry out his plan. Alexander set out to conquer an empire.

MACEDON
BLACK SEA
CASPIAN SEA
Alexandria
GREECE
Issus
ASIA
Area conquered by Alexander
MEDITERRANEAN SEA
SYRIA
Babylon
Tyre
Persepolis
Alexandria
Siwa
PERSIAN GULF
INDIA
EGYPT
RED SEA

Alexander was educated in the Greek way by Aristotle, the philosopher, and was a tough soldier, like all Macedonians.

Alexander crossed into Asia with his army and defeated the Persian king Darius III at the battle of Issus in 333BC. The Roman mosaic pictured above, is a copy of a Greek painting showing Alexander at Issus.

Alexander moved through the Persian empire to Syria. The Phoenician city of Tyre was attacked with catapults on boats.

Oasis of Siwa

Egypt was easily conquered. Alexander was hailed as the son of the god Ammon. Some Greeks disapproved of this.

Alexander led his army through difficult, mountainous country.

Alexander fought Darius again and defeated him in 331BC. Then he led his army through to Persepolis.

Alexander's army captured and looted the Persian king's treasure stored at Persepolis, then set off towards India.

In India, they won many battles, including one against King Porus, in which they met war elephants for the first time.

Alexander was buried in Alexandria.

Alexander died of a fever in 323BC on the long trek home from India. His body was taken to Alexandria in Egypt.

Alexandria

Alexander founded many cities, all called Alexandria, after him. The greatest of all was on the Mediterranean coast of Egypt. It became one of the most splendid cities of the ancient world. Alexander's general Ptolemy, became King of Egypt and founded the Mouseion, a place where scholars could meet, talk and do scientific experiments. There was also a magnificent library containing many valuable books. Ptolemy's family ruled Egypt for 300 years.

Bronze mirrors at the top reflected the light.

The Pharos

Many buildings were of Greek design with columns and statues.

Some Egyptian monuments like this obelisk, were also erected.

The lighthouse of Alexandria, the Pharos, was one of the wonders of the world. Alexandrian merchants sailed to India and the East, bringing back spices and silks for sale in the Mediterranean world.

Science and inventions

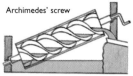
Archimedes' screw

Many things were invented in Alexandria. Archimedes is said to have designed this screw, which lifts water from one level to another. It is still used today.

The Alexandrians were interested in geography. This is the scientist Eratosthenes who used the angle of the sun's shadow to work out the distance round the Earth.

An astronomer called Ptolemy studied the planets from Alexandria. He believed the Earth was the centre of the universe as shown in this diagram.

Ptolemy's Earth

Siege catapult

Stone

Twisted rope made of animal sinew or human hair

Alexander's military engineers designed catapults which hurled stones, for attacking walled cities. Later, the Romans used catapults in their sieges too.

How to make a catapult

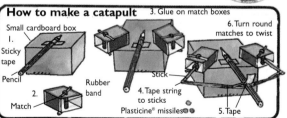

Small cardboard box
1.
Sticky tape
Pencil
Match
2.
Rubber band
3. Glue on match boxes
Stick
4. Tape string to sticks
Plasticine® missiles
5. Tape
6. Turn round matches to twist

(1) Tape a pencil to a small box, like this. (2) Make holes through two match box covers, push through short rubber bands. Slide match sticks through them. (3) Glue the covers to the box.

(4) Push two sticks into the bands. Tape string to the ends. (5) Tape the string on each side of the pencil and a bit of card on top. (6) Wind round the match sticks. Load and pull back to fire.

What we owe the Greeks

We know more about the Greeks than many earlier people, because they wrote proper histories. Other people listed kings' names and events, but did not explain things. The Greek historian, Herodotus, wrote studies of people and their customs. Thucydides, who fought in the Peloponnesian War, wrote a detailed history. We have inherited many things from the Greeks, including ideas of politics, theatre and many words.

The Greeks developed the art of thinking about problems. They called this philosophy. Two of the world's greatest philosophers, Socrates and Plato lived in Athens.

Some scholars, like Aristotle, studied scientific problems. He carefully watched animals and realised that the porpoise was a mammal not a fish, when he saw it give birth to live babies.

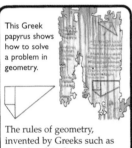

This Greek papyrus shows how to solve a problem in geometry.

The rules of geometry, invented by Greeks such as Euclid and Pythagoras are still used today.

The Olympic Games

Greek festivals, or "games", held in honour of the gods included sports, music and drama competitions. There were games at Corinth and Delphi, but the most famous were the Olympic Games held every four years at the sanctuary of the god Zeus in Olympia. The competitors had to be free Greeks, not slaves. They swore an oath to keep the rules. All wars in Greece had to stop during the games. Afterwards, oxen were sacrificed to Zeus and everyone joined in a great feast.

The Greeks studied plants. Manuscripts, like the one above, record recipes for medicines made of plants.

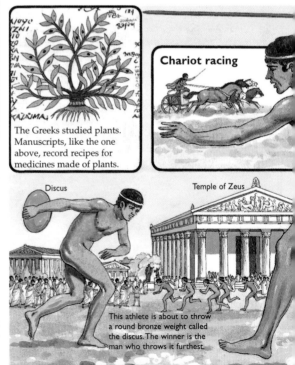

Chariot racing

Discus

Temple of Zeus

This athlete is about to throw a round bronze weight called the discus. The winner is the man who throws it furthest.

Art and architecture

When the Romans conquered Greece, their generals carried off many works of art. The Romans admired the Greek statues so much that they had marble copies made.

After the fall of the Roman empire, statues were buried and lost. In the 15th century AD, people began to be interested in the ancient world and dug up the remains.

From then on, architects throughout Europe revived Greek and Roman styles of building. Today, most cities have some public buildings which are in the "Classical" style.

Throwing the javelin. It was hurled from a leather thong wrapped round the athlete's fingers.

Four-horse racing was part of the Olympic Games. It took place on a separate race-track called the hippodrome. The Romans took over this exciting sport from the Greeks.

Judge with his official rod

This is a sprint race. There were also races run by men wearing full armour.

Wrestling

Spot the columns

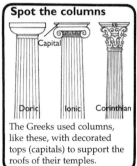

Capital

Doric Ionic Corinthian

The Greeks used columns, like these, with decorated tops (capitals) to support the roofs of their temples.

Key dates

499	Ionian Greeks revolted against Persian rule.
490	Start of Persian wars. Persians defeated at Battle of Marathon.
480	Greeks defeated at Thermopylae, then victorious at Salamis.
478/477	Athens led league of Greek states.
462/429	**Pericles**, leader at Athens.
431/404	**Peloponnesian War** between Sparta and Athens.
338	**Philip II** of Macedon won control of Greece.
336/323	**Reign of Alexander the Great**. During this time Alexander won a huge empire. On his death, the empire was divided up by his successors.

Approximate BC dates

73

Great civilisation in the East

Until 221BC, China was divided into several rival states. Then, the king of a state called Ch'in defeated them all and became the First Emperor of all China. "Shih Huang Ti", as he was called, was the first of a family line of emperors (a dynasty) called the Ch'in emperors. Later, the Han dynasty ruled China. At this time, General Chang Chien was sent to the West to find allies and a new trade route, called the Silk Road, was opened up.

Key dates

551/479BC	The great thinker **Confucius**.
463/221BC	Period of the warring states.
221BC	China unified under **Shih Huang Ti**, the First Emperor. Great Wall built. Beginning of Ch'in Dynasty. Standard bronze coins introduced.
206BC/AD220	Han Dynasty
200BC	Paper invented. Beginnings of Chinese civil service.

These dates are approximate

When the people of China were counted in AD2, there were about 60 million. Most were peasants who grew rice, their most important crop.

Great lords had tombs built for themselves for a comfortable life-after-death. This princess's body was covered with jade. It was thought to preserve it.

The emperor controlled salt wells, which were vital to people who lived far from the sea. Bamboo tubes were drilled down 400 metres into the brine.

How we know

Peasant's cottage

Peasant girl

We can learn about life at the time of the Han emperors from the pottery models placed in tombs. This is a one-storey house a peasant might live in.

Farm

Watch tower

Farm animals

Bronze figure of a tall Western horse

Even a farm needed towers to watch for barbarians or soldiers. A rich lord had models of servants and soldiers in his tomb to impress the gods.

General Chang Chien brought a new breed of horse from the West. The big, strong horses were useful against the small ponies ridden by barbarians.

The Great Wall

The Great Wall of China was built by Shih Huang Ti when he became emperor. He joined together short sections of wall put up by earlier warlords to keep raiding tribes out of their lands. The wall still stands and is 2,710km long.

Beacons on the watch towers signal the approach of an enemy

A convoy on the Silk Road is halted by an attack.

Chinese cross-bowman

Barbarians on their swift ponies.

The wall is wide enough to take chariots.

Silk

Silkworm

Sorting cocoons

The Chinese made and sold fine silk. They kept silk worms, which spin cocoons of silk thread. They dyed and wove this silk into cloth.

Patterns of plants and animals were woven into the silk. This lion pattern may have been borrowed from Persia, which shows ideas, as well as goods, were taken along the Silk Road.

Money

Fish money

Standard money

Silk

Silk was so valuable it was used for payment. Bronze coins in strange shapes were also used. Later, round coins with square holes became standard money.

Writing and inventions

The Chinese emperor was treated like a god. He had armies of officials and soldiers to run his empire. The officials – civil servants – collected taxes and looked after roads.

Any boy who could read and write had a chance of being a civil servant. But he had to know large amounts of ancient poetry and the teachings of the great thinker, Confucius.

Confucius, born in 551BC, taught that the emperor should be like a father to his people, who should obey him. Confucius scholars had to be good at music, arithmetic, archery and chess too.

Chinese character for book

Old Chinese book made of strips of bamboo

The writing used in China today is thousands of years old. Each character was based on a picture which gradually became simple brush strokes.

The ancient Chinese wrote and painted on long pieces of silk. They used Chinese brushes and ground up a solid block of ink on stone with a little water.

The Chinese painted pictures in beautiful colours. In a corner, they often put characters, based on things in the picture, such as "mountain" and "river".

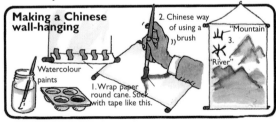

Making a Chinese wall-hanging

Watercolour paints

1. Wrap paper round cane. Stick with tape like this.

2. Chinese way of using a brush

3. "Mountain" "River"

Inventions

You will need a sheet of paper. (1) Fasten cane to each end with sticky tape. (2) Hold your brush in the Chinese way and paint a landscape.

(3) Next copy the Chinese characters. These are the characters for "river" and "mountain". Together, they mean "landscape".

The Chinese wrote on silk or in bamboo books, then began to make paper from bark and hemp. They used this to paint, write and take rubbings from stone tablets.

Life in the city

All the cities built at the time of the Han emperors have disappeared. This picture of their capital city, Ch'ang-An, is based on paintings, sculptures and tomb figures from the time.

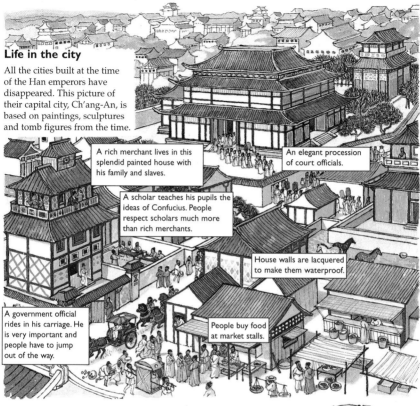

A rich merchant lives in this splendid painted house with his family and slaves.

An elegant procession of court officials.

A scholar teaches his pupils the ideas of Confucius. People respect scholars much more than rich merchants.

House walls are lacquered to make them waterproof.

A government official rides in his carriage. He is very important and people have to jump out of the way.

People buy food at market stalls.

The Chinese invented the first compass. A spoon-shaped piece of magnetic stone, called lodestone, was placed on a polished bronze board. The spoon turned until it pointed to the North Pole.

The Chinese covered wooden bowls and boxes with layers of sticky resin, called lacquer, from the lac tree. They lacquered their shoes, chariots and umbrellas to make them waterproof and colourful.

This is an instrument for detecting earthquakes. The slightest tremor in the Earth tilts the carefully balanced mechanism inside. Then a dragon's jaws open and a ball falls into a toad's mouth.

Nomads and horsemen

Between the civilisations of the Mediterranean and China, were vast treeless plains and mountains. The tribes living there wandered great distances to find pasture for their horses and cattle.

One tribe, the Mongols, sometimes attacked the Great Wall of China. Another, the Scythians, were described by the Greek historian, Herodotus, as fine horsemen and archers. Russians digging in the Altai found tombs built about 500BC with objects preserved in ice.

MONGOLS

ALTAI

SCYTHS

ARAL SEA

BLACK SEA CASPIAN SEA

PERSIANS

CHINA

Zagros Mountains

Himalayas

RED SEA

PERSIAN GULF INDIA

Scythian horse-breeders

The Scythians of the Altai roamed the plains during the summer months but lived in log cabins during the winter. They sold horses from their huge herds to the Chinese and Persians.

The men round up horses to train them for riding and for carrying loads.

These men are making a coat of long-haired sheep skin. It will keep a man warm during the long, bitterly cold winter.

The warrior's thoroughbred horse is taller and faster than the herd horses. When its master dies, it will be buried with him.

The warrior's wife plaits ribbons into the horse's tail to decorate it. The saddle is covered with a soft, comfortable cushion.

Inside a Scythian cabin

In winter, the Scythians made things of felt and sewed on shapes, called appliqué. They also stitched embroidery. All their belongings could be packed on to horses when they moved.

How to do appliqué

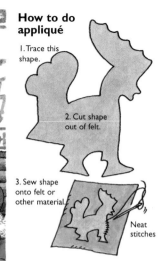

1. Trace this shape.

2. Cut shape out of felt.

3. Sew shape onto felt or other material.

Neat stitches

(1) Trace the shape of this Scythian cockerel. (2) Cut it out of coloured felt or material. (3) Stitch it to a large piece of felt or cloth. Sew on more cut-out shapes to make a wall-hanging.

Mongols

Mongols were true nomads and wandered the whole year round. Their tents, called yurts, were made of animal hair felt, waterproofed with fat.

Mongol chieftains had large, comfortably furnished yurts. They loaded them on to carts, pulled by oxen, when it was time to drive their herds on.

Lassoos on poles

When ponies were needed from the herd, men caught them. Most work was done by women, but the men did make a drink of mare's milk.

Water was so precious when travelling that no clothes or pots were allowed to be washed. Visitors had to walk between fires to be purefied.

How we know

The Scythians made things of gold, such as this plaque. It may show a warrior's death.

The Mongols made whistles to join to arrows so they could hear where an arrow fell.

Early Native Americans

The first Native Americans ate seeds and berries, and followed herds of wild animals. Later, they began to build more permanent homes and grow crops near them.

Some, like the Hopewell people, built large cemeteries for their dead. In Central America, Native Americans built pyramids, at first, faced with clay, then with stone slabs. Ideas spread between North America and Mexico, when they traded with each other.

NORTHERN FOREST TRIBES

NORTH AMERICA

TRIBES OF THE GREAT PLAINS

EASTERN WOODLAND TRIBES

SOUTH WEST DESERT TRIBES

•Serpent mound

SOUTH WEST MESA TRIBES

SOUTH EAST AND FLORIDA TRIBES

ATLANTIC OCEAN

Teotihuacan•

MEXICO

OLMECS

PACIFIC OCEAN

MAYA

•Copan

The Native Americans of the desert lived in caves and went out hunting for wild sheep. They wove elaborate baskets and made moccasins of skins.

On plains and in woodlands, the Native Americans lived in shallow pit houses, covered with hides. A holy man, called a shaman, chanted spells to cure ill people.

Some woodland tribes built mounds of earth in the shape of animals. This snake was made by Hopewell people 2,000 years ago. It is about 500 metres long.

Olmec Indians in Central America built huge stone statues. They thought their jaguar-god mated with women, who had half-jaguar babies.

A city of pyramids was built at Teotihuacan, Central Mexico. Round the city, fields of maize, beans and pumpkins fed about 200,000 people who lived there.

Maize plant

Native North Americans learned how to grow tobacco and maize from people in Central America. The maize was so good, they made it a god.

The Maya

The Maya Indians of Central America built cities which can still be seen deep in the jungle. They were religious and worshipped rain, earth, plant and animal gods. They played a religious ball game in specially built courts. Priests kept the score.

The Maya studied the moon, stars and planets, and had a complicated calendar to count days and years. They wanted to predict when frightening things, like an eclipse of the sun would happen.

How to play hip ball

Two equal teams

Big ball

Line on ground

A player tosses the ball over the line. The teams hit it across the line, using only hips, thighs and elbows. A point is scored against the one who lets it drop. The first to score 21 wins the game.

The ball court at Copan

The ball court at Copan was probably built late in the eighth century AD. The players, bandaged to prevent injuries, used a solid rubber ball.

They bounced the ball backwards and forwards, using only their hips, thighs and elbows, but not their feet. No one really knows how they scored goals.

How we know

We know little about how Maya people lived. This tomb painting shows they fought their neighbours, probably to capture people to sacrifice to the gods.

The Maya were very good stone carvers. These masons are working on a pillar, probably showing a king. It will be set up to mark an important date.

Mayan potters made amazing clay pots. They coiled strips of clay round and round, to build up the pot. This man is turning the pot round with his feet.

Life in ancient Africa

The first people lived in Africa about three million years ago. From the great civilisations of Egypt, other Africans learned how to work gold, copper, tin and bronze. The Assyrians, with iron weapons, invaded the Nile valley in 671BC. The use of iron spread. Two powerful kingdoms grew up south of Egypt – Kush and Axum (modern Ethiopia). Christianity was brought to Ethiopia by Egyptian monks. King Ezana was one of the first rulers to become a Christian.

Key dates

1000BC	Beginnings of Kingdom of Kush. Capital at Napata.
751/664BC	Kushite kings conquered and ruled Egypt.
671BC	The Assyrians invaded the Nile Valley.
590BC	Capital of Kush moved from Napata to Meroe.
AD339	Meroe conquered by King Ezana of Axum.

These dates are approximate

Some of Africa's earliest history can be seen in paintings on the walls of caves. This picture, based on a rock painting, shows a battle between small bushmen and tall Bantu warriors. Such battles forced the weaker tribes to move their herds and villages to new areas where no people had lived before.

The capital of Kush was at Napata until about 590BC. A new capital was built at Meroe, near iron deposits. It had pyramids like those in Egypt.

The use of iron may have spread from Kush westwards across Africa. Blacksmiths were important as they knew how to make weapons.

The North African coast had been settled by Phoenicians and Greeks. The Romans then went further inland. Nomads in the hills learned to trade at markets.

At the port of Adulis, the traders of Axum exchanged African ivory for spices from India and Ceylon, and cloth from the Roman empire.

Buddha and Ashoka

People called Aryans moved into India in about 1750BC but little is known of India's history at that time. After the conquests of Alexander the Great in Northern India and Pakistan, a line of kings, the Mauryans, built a great empire. They learned ideas of government from the Greeks and Persians. Ashoka, a Mauryan conqueror, was converted to Buddhism and made it the state religion. Beautiful sculpture and art developed under the next strong line of kings, the Guptas.

Key dates

560/480BC	**Gautama** (The Buddha)
327/325BC	Campaigns of Alexander the Great in India and Pakistan.
321/185BC	The Mauryan Dynasty founded by **Chandragupta**.
272/231BC	**Ashoka**, grandson of Chandragupta, was emperor. Capital city at Pataliputra (modern Patna). Buddhism spread through India.
AD320/535	The Gupta empire.
AD400/500	The Ajanta frescoes were painted.

Vishnu, one of the many Hindu gods

The Aryans' religion was Hinduism. Priests taught that the gods decided which way of life, or caste, a person was born into.

There were four castes, but many people were too lowly to be in any of them. They were called "untouchables" and did the worst jobs.

The high caste rulers of India lived in luxury in their palaces. This fresco, painted on a cave wall at Ajanta in about AD400, shows the inside of a palace.

Buddha

Gautama, a young prince, was so moved when he saw suffering, he left his palace to find a better way of life.

He thought out a kinder religion and became known as the Buddha, meaning the enlightened one.

Buddha's ideas spread. Later, earth mounds, called stupas, were built where he had preached.

Top of one of Ashoka's columns

Buddha's teachings were adopted by Emperor Ashoka. He made fairer laws, written on stone columns.

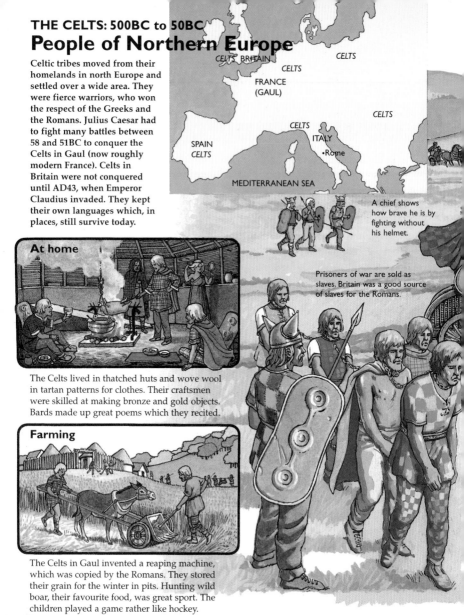

THE CELTS: 500BC to 50BC
People of Northern Europe

Celtic tribes moved from their homelands in north Europe and settled over a wide area. They were fierce warriors, who won the respect of the Greeks and the Romans. Julius Caesar had to fight many battles between 58 and 51BC to conquer the Celts in Gaul (now roughly modern France). Celts in Britain were not conquered until AD43, when Emperor Claudius invaded. They kept their own languages which, in places, still survive today.

CELTS BRITAIN

CELTS

FRANCE
(GAUL)

CELTS

CELTS

SPAIN
CELTS

ITALY
•Rome

MEDITERRANEAN SEA

A chief shows how brave he is by fighting without his helmet.

Prisoners of war are sold as slaves. Britain was a good source of slaves for the Romans.

At home

The Celts lived in thatched huts and wove wool in tartan patterns for clothes. Their craftsmen were skilled at making bronze and gold objects. Bards made up great poems which they recited.

Farming

The Celts in Gaul invented a reaping machine, which was copied by the Romans. They stored their grain for the winter in pits. Hunting wild boar, their favourite food, was great sport. The children played a game rather like hockey.

In Northern Europe, the Celts built huge hill forts. Here they were safe from attacks by other tribes or the Romans.

Hill fort

Huts and cattle enclosures

The warriors ride chariots into battle. They dismount to fight with their swords.

Some young Celts have hired themselves out as mercenary soldiers. They fight naked to show how courageous they are.

How we know

This shield was probably used only for display. The wooden leg was put in a stream so a goddess would heal the real leg.

Religion

The Celts had priests, called Druids. It took many years to become a Druid. He had to train his memory to learn, and hand on, laws and customs.

Human skulls were placed in this monument at Roquepertuse, France. Human remains, maybe from sacrifices, have been found in pits at some religious centres.

Later Celts became Christians. They set up communities of monks in Scotland. Some, such as St Columba, were sent to convert the heathens.

The rise of Rome

1. The city of Rome began as a small village on one of seven hills. More villages were built until they joined up into one big town.

2. At first, Rome was ruled by kings. Later, the people rebelled and set up a "republic" (a state without a king).

3. The Romans conquered other peoples in Italy. They fought the Carthaginians whose leader, Hannibal invaded Italy in 218BC.

4. Men who fought for Rome settled down to farm the land they had conquered and brought the Roman way of life to the provinces.

5. People captured in battle were made slaves. One called Spartacus, was trained as a gladiator. In 71BC, he led a slave revolt.

The Etruscans

Etruscan man and woman from top of coffin.

Etruscan people lived in central Italy. Little is known about them as their writings cannot be read. Their sculpture shows Greek influence.

Roman roads

Flat stones

Rubble

Stones

Ditch

Roman soldiers built thousands of miles of good roads. Troops could march quickly along them to control their huge empire.

The end of the Republic

1. In Rome, many men plotted to gain control. There were civil wars. Julius Caesar, a great general, marched his army to Rome in 49BC.

2. Caesar soon gained power and brought peace. One group, fearing he planned to make himself king, stabbed him to death.

3. Octavian, Caesar's heir, defeated his rival, Mark Antony. Antony and his wife, Cleopatra, Queen of Egypt, killed themselves.

4. Octavian was given the title Augustus. He became the first Roman Emperor. He restored order in the army and revived Roman customs.

The Roman army

The well-trained Roman armies spread outwards from Rome, gradually winning more and more territory. The soldiers laid siege to enemy forts, marching up to the walls under a roof of shields. They built wooden towers to scale the walls and broke down gates with a battering ram. When marching through enemy lands, the soldiers set up a camp each night. They rounded up animals and cut crops for food.

They used catapults to fling stones on to defenders. A soldier carried the standard which was crowned by the legion's eagle.

Life in the Roman Empire

The rule of Emperor Augustus brought an end to the Roman republic with elected leaders. In its place, a peaceful empire was set up.

Inside the well-guarded Roman frontiers, new cities grew up where no towns had been before. From Britain to North Africa, fine temples and houses of brick or stone were built. The people in the provinces traded for the goods they needed and paid government taxes for the upkeep of the army.

In the cities, fresh water was brought from the hills by aqueducts. Then it flowed along lead pipes to street fountains and houses. There were baths where people could wash and swim. Food and wine were shipped from the provinces to the city docks.

Streets were paved with stone and had drains to keep them clean.

Aqueduct

Baths

Wheat from the provinces

Statue of emperor

Gladiator fights

People flocked to arenas called amphitheatres to watch fights to the death between gladiators and wild animals or condemned criminals.

Country life

There were many towns and cities, but most people lived in the country. Rich men had large estates, looked after by farmers who paid them rent with money, food or animals. On the estates were grand houses, called villas, where rich families lived with their servants and slaves. Workers grew wheat, vegetables, fruit, grapes for making wine, and olives for oil. They kept hens, geese, cows, sheep and goats. Oil and wine were stored in jars half-buried in the courtyard.

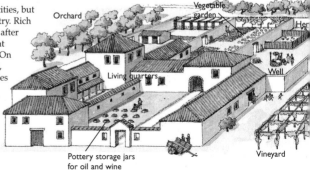

Orchard

Vegetable garden

Her

Living quarters

Well

Vineyard

Pottery storage jars for oil and wine

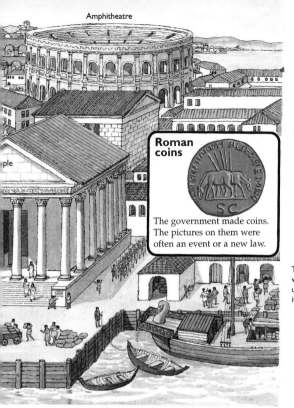

Amphitheatre

Roman coins

The government made coins. The pictures on them were often an event or a new law.

Pompeii

1. The volcano, Mount Vesuvius, towers over the Bay of Naples in Italy. In AD79, it erupted, sending fumes and ashes onto the towns at its base. The city of Pompeii was buried by rivers of scorching lava. Archaeologists have dug through the lava and found the city, is preserved in great detail.

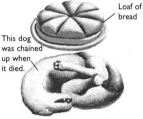

Loaf of bread

This dog was chained up when it died.

2. The shape of a round loaf of bread, still on a plate, was preserved by the lava. Some people and animals choked to death in the fumes.

Mosaics were used to decorate the floors of the villas. Often they showed scenes from country life, like this farmer digging the soil around his grape vines.

Ordinary people had little of their own. They grew food on rented land for their families and for sale. This man is driving his cow to a city market.

3. Many houses, with coloured paintings on their walls, have been found under the lava. This is a portrait of a woman who lived there.

Romans and barbarians

After Augustus, the Roman empire was ruled by strong emperors. Armies guarded its frontiers and many people became its citizens. From the time of Emperor Marcus Aurelius, however, the empire was troubled by barbarian invasions. The Roman armies grew more powerful and began to set up their own leaders as emperors, which led to civil wars. Eventually, Emperor Diocletian divided the empire into four parts, each with its own capital city.

1. Emperor Hadrian had forts, linked by a huge wall, built across northern England to keep out the barbarians.

2. The Persians attacked the frontiers, led by Shapur. Emperor Valerian marched against him but was defeated.

3. The emperors tried to pay for larger armies by minting extra money. Bronze coins were coated with silver to look more valuable.

4. People tried to blame the Christians for the empire's troubles because they would not worship Roman gods. Thousands were killed in arenas.

5. Tribes searching for new land invaded Northern Italy. Emperor Aurelian drove them out and had walls built round Rome.

Jews in Palestine rebelled against the Romans, who destroyed Jerusalem in AD70. Some Jews hid their religious writings in caves near the Dead Sea.

Some people in Palestine followed a religious leader called Jesus. They were known as Christians because he was called Christ, the Messiah.

Christians used secret symbols. The fish meant Christ. The Chi-rho sign is the first two letters of Christ in Greek. The palm leaf means victory over death.

The empire splits up

Statue of the Tetrarchs which now stands in Venice

1. Wars on several frontiers made the empire difficult to control. Emperor Diocletian divided it into four parts, each with a ruler, or "tetrarch".

2. Diocletian's successors fought for power. Constantine beat his rival at the Milvian Bridge. He had dreamed he would win if he carried the Christian symbol.

3. Constantine then became a Christian and set up a new capital, called after him at Byzantium. Later Emperor Theodosius II built walls round it.

The barbarians

1. People in the Roman empire asked barbarians to protect them against other barbarians. But the attacks went on. In Britain, forts and look-out towers were built to guard the coasts.

2. Roman emperors, in need of good soldiers, paid barbarians to lead their armies. Stilicho, a Vandal, commanded all troops and married the niece of Theodosius I.

3. The fiercest barbarians, the Huns, came from central Asia and had driven many people into Roman lands. Their leader, Attila, was called "the scourge of God".

Buried treasure

The Romans often buried their treasures to hide them from attacking barbarians. These Christian silver objects, which are about 1,600 years old, were dug up in a field in England.

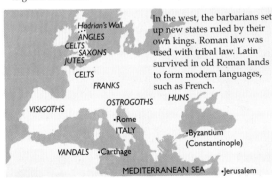

In the west, the barbarians set up new states ruled by their own kings. Roman law was used with tribal law. Latin survived in old Roman lands to form modern languages, such as French.

Hadrian's Wall
ANGLES
CELTS
SAXONS
JUTES
CELTS
FRANKS
OSTROGOTHS
HUNS
VISIGOTHS
•Rome
ITALY
•Byzantium
(Constantinople)
VANDALS •Carthage
MEDITERRANEAN SEA •Jerusalem

The Byzantine Empire

The city of Constantinople resisted attacks by barbarians and became the capital of the eastern half of the Roman empire. This eastern empire lasted for more than 1,000 years and is called the Byzantine empire.

In the sixth century AD, some land captured by the barbarians was won back. The armies of Emperor Justinian regained Italy from the Ostrogoths and North Africa from the Vandals. But there were costly wars with the rival Persian empire.

The court of Justinian

Justinian's wife, Theodora was a clever and powerful woman who helped rule.

The imperial guards have Christian signs on their shields.

Silk for robes worn by rich people came only from China. The Persians made trade difficult. Monks, so the story goes, brought silk worms to Justinian to start a silk industry.

Mosaics

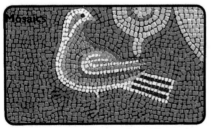

The Romans decorated the walls and floors of their houses with small cubes of coloured stone. These are called mosaics. At the time of Justinian, coloured glass, sometimes with gold set in it, was used, and even precious stones.

How to make a mosaic

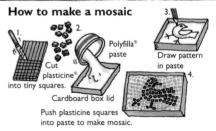

1.
2.
Cut plasticine® into tiny squares.
Polyfilla® paste
Cardboard box lid
Push plasticine squares into paste to make mosaic.
3.
Draw pattern in paste
4.

(1) Roll out plasticine® and cut it into squares. Mix Polyfilla® with water to make a thick paste. (2) Pour it into a small box lid. (3) Draw a picture in the paste. (4) Before the paste sets, push the squares into it to make a mosaic, like this.

Chariot race

Many customs were brought from Rome. Chariot racing in the circus became mixed with politics. In a great riot, 30,000 supporters of the Blue and Green parties were killed.

The earliest Christian monks built monasteries in Egypt. Some wanted to live alone in great discomfort to prove their faith. One monk, Simon, spent years on a pillar.

In the monasteries, monks copied out manuscripts of Christian writings and older Greek works. They kept up the skills of painting ikons (images) of holy people.

Barbarian kingdoms

KINGDOM OF THE FRANKS

KINGDOM OF THE VISIGOTHS

OSTROGOTHS

ITALY Rome Constantinople

BYZANTINE EMPIRE at the time of Justinian

MEDITERRANEAN SEA

King Recceswinth's crown

His name

Justinian's empire is shown here. In the west are the beginnings of several European kingdoms. The Franks have settled in France and Germany and the Visigoths in Spain.

The Visigoths were a Germanic people. The crown in this picture was put in a church as an offering by King Recceswinth. It may have been made by Byzantine craftsmen.

The Ostrogoths settled in Italy and were finally defeated by Justinian. They made jewellery in eagle designs. The Anglo-Saxon gold cross was worn as a Christian symbol.

Key dates

753BC	Traditional date of founding of Rome.
575BC	Rome ruled by Etruscan kings.
509BC	Romans set up republic.
264/241BC	First war with Carthage.
218BC	Second war with Carthage. **Hannibal** crosses the Pyrenees.
200BC	Rome began conquest of eastern Mediterranean.
146BC	Romans destroyed Carthage and Corinth.
73/71BC	**Spartacus** led slave revolt.
58/51BC	**Julius Caesar** conquered Celts in Gaul.
44BC	**Julius Caesar** murdered in Rome.
30BC	**Antony and Cleopatra** committed suicide.
27BC	**Octavian** called Augustus; beginning of Roman Empire.
AD14	Death of **Augustus**.
AD70	Temple at Jerusalem destroyed.
AD79	Eruption of Vesuvius; Pompeii destroyed.
AD117/38	**Hadrian** was emperor; built wall across north of England.
AD161/180	**Marcus Aurelius** was emperor.
AD235	Barbarian invasions and civil wars began.
AD249/250	First persecution of Christians under Emperor **Decius**.
AD270/275	**Aurelian** was emperor; built wall around city of Rome.
AD285/305	**Diocletian** was emperor.
AD312	**Constantine** won battle of Milvian Bridge.
AD330	Dedication of city of Constantinople.
AD395	Division of Roman empire into East and West.
AD527/565	**Justinian** was emperor.

93

Time Chart

First civilisations to the fall of Rome

	Mesopotamia and Persia	Egypt	Africa	Mediterranean lands of Europe
	Development of farming. Rise of city-states in Sumer. Pottery being made. Cuneiform writing invented. Wheel invented.	Development of farming. Pottery being made. Hieroglyphs invented.	Rock drawings in middle of Sahara showing animals and people.	Stone monuments built, e.g. in Malta.
3000BC	Early Dynastic period in Sumer. (First two dynasties of rulers.) Royal graves of Ur	Unification of Egypt. ARCHAIC PERIOD in Egypt. OLD KINGDOM. Step Pyramids built.		EARLY MINOAN PERIOD in Crete.
2500BC	**Sargon** of Akkad. The Gutians invade. Dynasty III or Ur.	Straight-sided Pyramids built.		
2000BC	Arrival of the Amorites. Rise of Babylon. Reign of King **Hammurabi** of Babylon. Rise of Assyria, under King **Shamsi-Adad I**.	MIDDLE KINGDOM. Conquest of Nubia. Invasion of Hyksos.		MIDDLE MINOAN PERIOD in Crete. Picture writing (hieroglyphs) in use in Crete. Palaces built in Crete. LATE MINOAN PERIOD in Crete.
1500BC	Kassites rule Babylon. The Mitanni rule in northern Mesopotamia. Arrival of the Persians.	NEW KINGDOM. Conquest of empire. Valley of Kings in use. Warrior pharoahs in power. **Queen Hatshepsut. Tutankhamun.**		Rise of Mycenaeans in Greece. Eruption of Thera. Linear B writing in use in Crete. Fall of Crete, destruction of Palace of Knossos.
1000BC	Rise and fall of ASSYRIAN EMPIRE. Rise of NEW BABYLONIAN EMPIRE. Rule of **Nebuchadnezzar** in Babylon. Birth of prophet **Zarathushtra**.	LATE PERIOD Slow decline. Invasion by Assyrians and Kushites. Egyptian revival.	Beginnings of Kingdom of Kush. Spread of iron working. Carthage founded by Phoenician princess **Dido**. Capital of Kush moved to Meroe.	Decline of Mycenaeans. Arrival of Dorians in Greece. Greek poet **Homer** alive. Etruscans in Northern Italy. Traditional date of founding of Rome 753BC. City-states in Greece.
500BC	PERSIAN EMPIRE at its height. Conquests of **Alexander the Great** (including Persian empire).	Conquest by Persia, then Alexander the Great. Rule of the Ptolemies. **Cleopatra.** Conquest by Rome.	Carthage at war with Rome (Punic wars). **Hannibal.** Carthage defeated. North Africa part of Roman empire.	Persian wars between Greeks and Persians.City of Athens very powerful. Peloponnesian War in Greece. Rule of **Pericles** in Athens. **Alexander the Great**. Rise of Rome. **Julius Caesar**.
0	SASSANIAN EMPIRE	Part of Roman Empire.	Meroe conquered by **King Ezana** of Axum. Slow movement of people across central and southern Africa. Arrival of barbarians (Vandals) in North Africa.	**Augustus**, Roman emperor. ROMAN EMPIRE Spread of Christianity. Split of Roman empire into West and East. BYZANTINE EMPIRE.
AD500		Hieroglyphs fall into disuse.		Byzantine empire ruled by Emperor **Justinian**.

Northern Europe	Western Asia	India	China	America
Stone monuments built in northern and western Europe.	First farmers. First cities – Jericho and Catal Hüyük.		Early farming communities growing millet.	
		Rise of Indus Valley People.		Farmers growing cotton. Maize grown in Mexico.
Stonehenge built. Spread of skilled bronze working.	Independent states in Anatolia. Arrival of Assyrian merchants for trade. Arrival of Canaanites in Eastern Mediterranean lands. Hittites arrive in Anatolia.	Cities like Mohenjo-Daro and Harappa built. Writing in use. Decline of Indus Valley people. Arrival of Aryan People.		Pottery being made.
Celts move across Europe.	HITTITE EMPIRE Arrival of Sea Peoples. Arrival of Israelites in Canaan. Philistines settle in Palestine. Israelites ruled by **King David**, then **King Solomon**. Their kingdom split into Israel and Judah. The Phoenicians prosper. Destruction of Jerusalem by Babylonians and people taken into captivity. Movement of Scythian horse breeders across Asia. Conquest of Eastern Mediterranean lands by **Alexander the Great**. Conquest by Romans. Birth of **Jesus Christ**. Destruction of Jerusalem by Romans. Area becomes part of Eastern Roman (Byzantine) Empire.	Development of caste system. Growth of Hindu religion. Vedas (religious writings). Birth of **Gautama (the Buddha)**. **Alexander the Great's** campaigns in India. MAURYAN DYNASTY founded by **Chandragupta**. **Ashoka** was emperor. Spread of Buddhism through India. GUPTA EMPIRE.	SHANG DYNASTY. Development of skilled bronze working. Royal tombs at Anyang. Development of writing in China. CHOU DYNASTIES. Birth of **Confucius**. Period of warring states. Unification of China under **Shih Huang Ti**. Great Wall built. CH'IN DYNASTY. HAN DYNASTY. Paper invented. Silk Road in use. End of Han Dynasty.	The Olmecs in Mexico. Rise of the Maya. Temples at Teotihuacan built.
Conquest of much of north Europe by Romans. Area becomes part of Roman empire. Barbarians attack Roman empire. Barbarian kingdoms set up in Britain, France and Germany.				

New kings in Persia

Persia was conquered in 331BC by the Greeks, led by Alexander the Great. After he died, a tribe called the Parthians took over and made their capital at Ctesiphon. Their warrior horsemen were a continual threat to the Romans.

In AD224, the Parthian king was overthrown by a new leader, who started the Sassanian line of kings. These kings lived and ruled in the style of the great Persian kings of the past.

The Sassanian kings built up a large empire. On their western frontier, they fought with the Romans. Shapur I scored a victory over the Romans in AD260, when he captured their emperor, Valerian.

All trade between East and West went through Persia, which became wealthy. Shapur I had a palace built at Bishapur. Silver bowls have been dug up, showing scenes of Sassanian life. This scene shows a banquet at the palace. The Sassanian empire collapsed in AD637 when Muslim Arabs invaded.

How Christianity survived

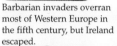

Monks living in small settlements in Ireland.

Barbarian invaders overran most of Western Europe in the fifth century, but Ireland escaped.

The Irish monks produced some beautiful books, written and decorated by hand. The page to the left is from the Book of Durrow.

Some monks set off from Ireland in tiny open boats to convert the heathens. One of the most famous is St Columba, who founded a settlement on the Island of Iona, off the west coast of Scotland.

The few Christians who remained in other parts of Western Europe also tried to convert people. One of the stories from this time tells of St Coifi, who lived in the north of England. He wanted to show the heathens how powerless their gods were, so he rode into one of their holy places and hurled his spear at the statues there. When the heathens saw that nothing dreadful happened, many decided that he was right and became Christians.

97

The beginning of a new religion

Soon after AD600*, in the land of Arabia, a man called Muhammad was preaching a new religion. He believed in Allah, the "One God". Most people in Arabia followed his religion and called him the Prophet. In Europe, most people in the Roman Empire were Christians. But, when the Empire was invaded, many began worshipping other gods. The eastern part of the Roman Empire (called the Byzantine Empire), was not invaded and stayed Christian.

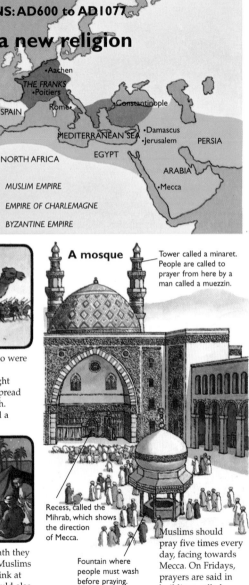

- THE FRANKS
  - Aachen
  - Poitiers
- SPAIN
- Rome
- Constantinople
- MEDITERRANEAN SEA
- Damascus
- Jerusalem
- PERSIA
- NORTH AFRICA
- EGYPT
- ARABIA
- Mecca

MUSLIM EMPIRE

EMPIRE OF CHARLEMAGNE

BYZANTINE EMPIRE

Islam Page from Koran

The teachings of Muhammad were written in a book called the Koran. His faith was known as Islam. His followers were called Muslims.

The caliphs, who were Muhammad's successors, fought many wars to spread the Muslim faith. They conquered a great empire.

Muslims going to Mecca.

All Muslims are meant to make a pilgrimage to Mecca, the home of Muhammad, at least once in their lives.

During the month they call Ramadan, Muslims only eat and drink at night. They should also give money to the poor.

A mosque

Tower called a minaret. People are called to prayer from here by a man called a muezzin.

Recess, called the Mihrab, which shows the direction of Mecca.

Fountain where people must wash before praying.

Muslims should pray five times every day, facing towards Mecca. On Fridays, prayers are said in buildings called mosques, like this.

Christians in Europe

The Pope with a priest.

1. The Christian Church in western Europe was led by the Pope. Many popes sent out missionaries to persuade people to become Christians.

2. Some missionaries were killed by the people they tried to convert. It was several hundred years before people in Europe accepted Christianity.

3. Muslims began to invade southern Europe. In AD732, Charles Martel, king of a people called the Franks, defeated them at the Battle of Poitiers.

4. This is Roderigo of Bivar, known as El Cid, which means "The Lord". He helped keep Muslims out of northern Spain and became a great Christian hero.

This gold image of Charlemagne was made to put his skull in.

5. In AD768, Charlemagne (Charles the Great) became King of the Franks. He conquered a lot of Europe and became its first great leader since the Roman Empire.

6. Charlemagne made the people he conquered become Christians, and fought the Muslims in Spain. On Christmas Day AD800, Pope Leo III crowned him Holy Roman Emperor.

7. After Charlemagne's death, his empire was divided. Holy Roman Emperors ruled only the German-speaking peoples of Europe from then on, but were still very powerful.

8. Emperors and popes often quarrelled over power. Once, Pope Gregory VII kept Henry IV waiting in the snow outside Canossa Castle for three days before he would forgive him. Quarrels between other emperors and popes resulted in long wars.

Key dates

AD570/632	Life of **Muhammad**.
AD622	First year of the Muslim calendar.
AD630	Mecca surrendered to Mohammad.
AD635	Muslims captured Damascus.
AD637/642	Muslims conquered Persia.
AD638	Muslims captured Jerusalem.
AD641/642	Muslims conquered Egypt.
By AD700	All North Africa conquered by Muslims.
AD732	Battle of Poitiers.
AD768/814	Reign of **Charlemagne**.
AD800	**Charlemagne** crowned Holy Roman Emperor.
AD1077	Meeting at Canossa between **Henry IV** and **Gregory VII**.
AD1043/1099	Life of **El Cid**.

Life in Viking times

In Norway, Sweden and Finland people called Norsemen lived. They were farmers, fishermen and traders. Norsemen who sailed abroad were called Vikings. Some settled in France and became known as Normans.

Wooden houses

Burial mounds

Wooden cart

Fishermen returning home

Chief's hall

A few animals spend the winter in their owner's house. The rest were killed in the autumn and the meat salted to make it keep.

Carving walrus tusks

Bed

Sledge

Wooden bucket

Vikings lived in settlements like this one. The wall and part of the roof of the chief's house have been cut away so that you can see inside.

Carvings

The Vikings were skilled wood-carvers and metal-workers. This carved wooden head is from a wagon.

Runes

Memorial stones to the dead were sometimes set up. These usually had letters called runes carved on them.

A burial

This is the grave of a Viking warrior. Later it will be covered with earth. His possessions, including his animals and sometimes even a slave, were buried with him. The Vikings believed that dead warriors went to "Valhalla", the hall of the gods.

Viking Raiders

When they are out of sight of land, they steer by the Pole Star and the Sun.

The men row when they are setting off and landing when there is not enough wind for sailing.

Ropes at bottom corners turn the sail to catch the wind.

Steering oar

The Vikings were adventurers, sailors and warriors. At first, they plundered other lands. Later they settled in parts of Europe, including Iceland.

From Iceland, they went to Greenland and from there they may have reached America. Long poems, called sagas, were written about Viking heroes.

Vikings in France (Normans) were great soldiers. William, Duke of Normandy conquered England in AD1066. Others conquered Sicily and part of Italy.

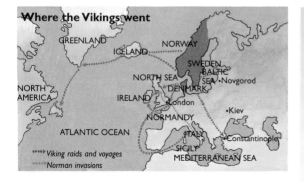

Where the Vikings went

GREENLAND
ICELAND
NORWAY
SWEDEN
NORTH SEA
BALTIC SEA
•Novgorod
DENMARK
NORTH AMERICA
IRELAND
London
•Kiev
NORMANDY
ATLANTIC OCEAN
ITALY
•Constantinople
SICILY
MEDITERRANEAN SEA

····► Viking raids and voyages
····► Norman invasions

Key dates

AD793/900	Great Viking raids on British Isles and northern France.
AD862	Viking settlers in Kiev and Novgorod in Russia.
AD870/930	Iceland colonized by Vikings.
AD900/911	Normandy settled by Vikings.
AD960	**Harald Bluetooth**, King of Denmark, converted to Christianity.
AD1000	Vikings reached America.
AD1016	**Knut** became King of England.
AD1066	**William of Normandy** (William the Conqueror), descendant of Viking settlers, conquered England. Other Normans conquered part of Italy.

Kings, knights and castles

All the countries of Europe were organized in roughly the same way in the Middle Ages. A king or emperor ruled a whole country and owned all the land.

The king sometimes needed support or money for a particular plan. So he called a meeting of his nobles, bishops and specially chosen knights and townsmen to discuss it with him. This was the beginning of parliaments.

The king divided his land amongst his most important men. In return, they did "homage" to him. This meant that they knelt in front of him and promised to serve him and fight for him, whenever they were needed. These men were the nobles.

Each noble then divided his land among knights who did homage to him. Peasants served a noble or knight and in return, were allowed to live on his land. This arrangement of exchanging land for services is called the "feudal system".

Castles were uncomfortable places to live. They were damp, cold and draughty. Early castles had no glass in the windows and there was no running water. They were lit by torches made of twigs or rushes. Kings and nobles built castles to protect themselves against enemies. Two walls have been taken over, so you can see inside.

Travelling coach bringing guests.

Archers practising

Stables

Armour makers

1. A boy who wanted to be a knight was sent to a noble's house as a page. He was taught to fight and to behave.

2. When he was older he became a squire. It was his job to serve a knight and to follow him into battle.

3. If he proved himself worthy of the honour, a noble, perhaps the king, would "knight" the young man.

4. The knight's father or another noble gave him some land with peasants and villages, called a manor.

Becoming a knight

Chapel

Solar - private room of lord and his family.

Hawking party

Minstrels

Great Hall

Jester

Guardroom

Garden

Kitchen

Well

Dungeon

A joust

Coat-of-arms

Heralds

To practice for battle, knights took part in organized fights, called jousts. At a joust, two knights on horseback charged at each other with long lances and tried to knock each other to the ground. Each noble family had a "coat-of-arms", which was painted on their shields, so they could be recognized.

A knight wore a ribbon, badge or scarf belonging to his favourite lady. This was called her "favour". If he won, he brought great honour to her.

Village life

In the Middle Ages, most people in Europe lived in villages. Each village was controlled by the Lord of the Manor. It usually had three fields, divided into strips, which the lord allowed the villagers to farm. They paid him by giving him some of the food they grew.

All the peasants could use the common. They could graze their animals here and gather wood and berries.

The ford was a shallow part of the stream, where people could cross.

Fisherman. The Church said people should always eat fish on Fridays.

Ford

The villagers held fairs. This was their only chance to buy goods from outside the village. Jugglers, acrobats and musicians came to perform at fairs.

Priest's house

Dancing bear

Merchants came to the fair to buy the villagers' wool.

Wheat being harvested. Next year, they would grow barley in this field.

Black death

In AD1348, some sailors from the East arrived in Italy, bringing a terrible disease with them, known as the Plague or Black Death.

The Plague quickly spread across Europe, as people knew little about medicine. About one in every three people died from it.

The lord of the manor lived here in the Manor House.

Everyone had their grain ground into flour at the village mill.

Lord of the Manor going hunting. The peasants were forbidden to kill any game animals because that would spoil the lord's hunting.

Stray animals were put in a "pound" and their owners had to pay a fine before they could get them out.

Barley grew in this field. The next year, it would be left unplanted.

Ale house

Hole for smoke to come out.

Blacksmith

Stocks

Roof made of straw or reeds. This is called thatch.

Spinning wool

Tinker coming to the fair to mend and sell metal pots and pans.

Fields were left fallow (unplanted) for a year. This made them more fertile the next year.

105

Towns and trade

This is what towns looked like in the Middle Ages. The streets were made of earth or cobbles and were narrow and dirty. There were no underground drains so people threw their rubbish into the street. Rich merchants built their houses of stone but most houses were made of wood, so fire was always a great danger. Towns were very small by modern standards and were surrounded by high stone walls.

University

Picture sign shows what the shop sells.

As trade increased, townsmen wanted to organize their own affairs. The king or local lord gave many towns a charter.

Guilds

1. Each trade and craft had its own guild. The guild organized its members by fixing prices and standards of workmanship.

2. A boy who wanted to learn a trade was "apprenticed" to a master. He lived in his master's house and worked in his shop.

3. After seven years he made a special piece of work called a masterpiece. If it was good enough he could join the guild.

4. The mayor and corporation who ran the city, were chosen from the most important members of each of the guilds.

Mystery plays

5. As the population increased men could not find places as guild members so they had to work for others for wages.

On special holidays each guild acted different scenes from the Bible. These were called "mystery" plays. The guilds acted their

plays on wagons called pageants, which they moved around the town between each performance. Many people could not read

so the plays helped them get to know the stories in the Bible. In many towns the guild which did the best play won a prize.

Trade

The first bankers were rich merchants who lent money to people who wanted to organize trading expeditions.

Spices, jewels and silks were brought to Europe from India and China. Italian merchants controlled this trade.

Goods were carried overland by packhorses. Most roads were bad and there were often bandits in lonely areas.

Sea travel was also difficult and dangerous. Sailors steered by the stars and tried to keep close to the land.

The Church

The head of the Church in western Europe, the Pope, was elected by cardinals (the highest rank of priests) at a meeting called a conclave.

At one time there were three rival popes who all claimed to have been elected by a conclave. This argument was called the Great Schism.

Everyone went to church. All the services were in Latin, although only the priests and highly-educated people understood it.

Few people could read and write, except priests, so kings used them as secretaries and advisers. Priests of high rank were summoned to parliament.

No-one had discovered how to print books in Europe. All books were hand-written by monks and decorated with bright colours and gold leaf.

People who refused to believe the teachings of the Church were called heretics. Joan of Arc was burnt to death as a heretic. Later people decided she was a saint.

Bodies of saints or holy objects were put into jewelled containers called reliquaries. People respected them and worshipped in front of them.

Pilgrims

Some people went on journeys to holy places to show their devotion to God, to be forgiven for sins or cured of illness. These journeys were called pilgrimages.

Life in a nunnery

Some people chose to give their lives completely to God's service and to live apart from the rest of the world. Women who did this were called nuns and lived in nunneries. Men were called monks and lived in monasteries.

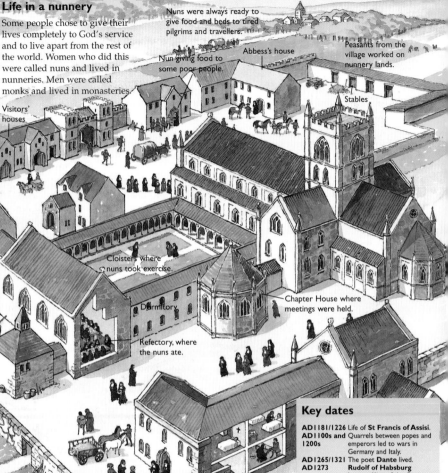

Nuns were always ready to give food and beds to tired pilgrims and travellers.

Nun giving food to some poor people.

Abbess's house

Peasants from the village worked on nunnery lands.

Visitors' houses

Stables

Cloisters where nuns took exercise.

Chapter House where meetings were held.

Dormitory

Refectory, where the nuns ate.

Hospice where nuns looked after people who are ill.

Nuns and monks promised to obey their superiors, to give up everything they owned and never to marry. Each day was divided into special times for prayer, study and work.

Like any Lord of the Manor, a nunnery had land. Rich people often left land and money to the nuns so they would pray for them. Some nunneries became extremely rich.

Key dates

AD1181/1226 Life of **St Francis of Assisi**.

AD1100s and 1200s Quarrels between popes and emperors led to wars in Germany and Italy.

AD1265/1321 The poet **Dante** lived.

AD1273 **Rudolf of Habsburg** became King of the Germans. His family ruled until 1918.

AD1307/1314 The Knights Templar were disbanded.

AD1337/1453 The **"Hundred Years"** War between France and England.

AD1370/1417 The Great Schism.

AD1380/1422 Quarrels between French nobles helped the English in the war.

AD1412/1431 Life of **Joan of Arc**. She led the French to victory in the war but was then burnt as a heretic.

Wars between religions

1. When invaders overran the western part of the Roman Empire, the eastern (Byzantine) half survived.

2. Over the years, eastern Christians of the Byzantine "Orthodox" Church, developed different beliefs from those of the west.

3. Between AD632 and 645, Muslims conquered part of the Byzantine Empire. This shows their caliph (ruler) entering Jerusalem.

4. Many Christian pilgrims visited the Holy Land, where Jesus had lived. The Muslims allowed them to continue these visits.

5. In the 11th century*, Seljuk Turks (Muslims), arrived in the area from the east. They were very unfriendly to the Christians.

6. When the Byzantines were defeated by the Turks at the Battle of Manzikert, western Christians felt they must protect the Holy Land.

The crusades

1. In AD1095, Pope Urban II gave a sermon at Clermont in France. He inspired people to go on a crusade (holy war).

2. The Crusaders set out on the long and difficult journey to the Holy Land to win it back from the Muslims. The leaders of the First Crusade were French noblemen, but their followers came from different countries.

3. Crusaders arrived in Constantinople and met the Emperor. At first he was friendly but he did not trust them.

110

4. The Crusaders went to fight the Muslims and were very successful. The Holy Land became a Christian kingdom, called Outremer.

5. Groups of soldier-monks were formed to care for pilgrims and to fight the Muslims. A knight from each of the most important groups is shown here.

Knight Templar

Teutonic Knight

Knight Hospitaller

6. Some Crusaders settled in Outremer. Crusaders who arrived were shocked that settlers were quarrelling with each other, but making friends with Muslims.

Saladin was a great leader.

7. The Muslims, under Saladin, won back Jerusalem from the quarrelling Christians. Several new crusades set out from Europe to try to win it back.

8. The feeling between European Crusaders and Byzantines grew so bad that some Crusaders attacked Constantinople itself and set up their own emperor.

Richard the Lionheart of England

9. St Louis of France, Richard the Lionheart and Frederick II of Germany tried to save Outremer. By AD1291, the Muslims had recaptured the Holy Land.

10. The Byzantines won back Constantinople but their days of power were over. In AD1453, with the help of cannons, the Turks finally captured the city.

How to spot a Crusader's tomb

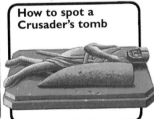

This is the tomb of a knight. His crossed legs show that he was a Crusader. Look out for a tomb like this if you go inside a cathedral or church.

Key dates

AD632/645	Muslims seized parts of Byzantine Empire.
AD638	Caliph Omar took Jerusalem.
AD1000/1100	Turks invaded Byzantine Empire.
AD1071	Battle of Manzikert.
AD1095	Sermon at Clermont.
AD1096	First Crusade, Jerusalem taken. Outremer founded.
AD1187	**Saladin** took Jerusalem.
AD1191	Crusade of **Richard the Lionheart**.
AD1204	Sack of Constantinople.
AD1228/1244	**Emperor Frederick II** won back Jerusalem for a while.
AD1249/1270	Crusades of **St Louis**.
AD 1261	Byzantine Emperor recaptured Constantinople.
AD1291	The end of Outremer.
AD1453	Turks captured Constantinople. (End of Byzantine Empire.)

*This means the 100 years between AD1000 and AD1100.

How Muslim people lived

The Arabs were the first Muslims and they conquered a huge empire. At first, the whole Muslim empire was ruled by one caliph, but later it split into several kingdoms. Life for the Muslims was often more advanced than life in Europe. After they had conquered the eastern provinces of the Roman Empire, they absorbed many of the ideas of ancient Greece and Rome. Trading made them wealthy, and this brought more comfort and luxury into their lives.

Arab nomads

Many Arabs were nomads who moved with their animals in search of water and pasture. They did not change their way of life after conquering their empire.

Peasants in Muslim lands went on working their fields. Much of the land was hot and dry and they had to work hard to keep it watered.

Muslim cities

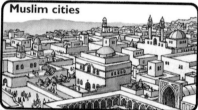

Houses in Muslim cities were often covered with white plaster, which helped to keep them cool. They faced inwards on to open courtyards, which provided shade. The streets were usually narrow and there were few open spaces except around the mosques.

Market

Towns usually had a souq (market). The streets where it was held were often roofed over. Shops in one street usually sold the same kind of goods.

Baths

Palaces, and many private houses, had baths and there were also public baths. They were copied from the designs of Roman baths.

Learning

Arabic writing

منـاذنـنـنـفـهـايـفـوقـكلـحـجـ

Arabic numbers

٠ ١ ٢ ٣ ٤ ٥ ٦ ٧ ٨ ٩

0 1 2 3 4 5 6 7 8 9
Our numbers

The Muslims developed a way of writing which read from right to left. Their system of numbers was simpler than the Roman figures used in Europe.

Muslim scholars studied the Greeks and Romans. They were interested in the stars, mathematics, geography, law, religion and medicine.

This instrument is called an astrolabe.

Arabs made instruments, like this one, which measured the position of ships at sea, by looking at the stars.

Muslim doctors followed ancient Greek methods of treating the sick. Hospitals were built to care for people needing treatment.

Hospital

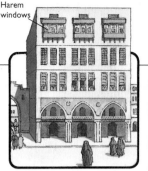

Muslim rulers built themselves huge palaces, like this one. These were beautifully decorated by skilled craftsmen and were very comfortable compared with European castles built at this time. They usually had gardens set out in patterns around fountains. Life in these palaces was very formal, with lots of ceremonies.

Harem windows

Part of a house was set aside for women only. This was called the harem. No man from outside the family could enter it. In the street, Muslim women wore veils.

Arab traders

Arab dhow

Trading played an important part in Muslim life. Arabs travelled to many different countries to find new customers. By sea, they travelled in fast ships, called dhows. Some Arabs still use dhows today.

On land, merchants travelled by camel in groups called caravans. On main routes, caravansarays (shelters) were built at a day's journey from each other. Travellers could spend the night there.

Muslim Art

Tiles

Their religion did not allow Muslim artists to make sculptures of the human figure. Instead, they used patterns, flowers, animals and birds as decoration.

Tiles were often used for decorating buildings. Muslim craftsmen were famous for the manufacture of beautiful carpets, and also for their metal work.

Carpet

Incense burner

This bronze lion was used for holding burning incense. Crusaders took treasures, like these, back west with them. The work of Muslim craftsmen became popular in Europe.

113

Genghis Khan and his Empire

The Mongols were nomads who wandered across the plains of Asia with their horses. From AD1206, a chief called Temujin conquered a huge empire. He became known as Genghis Khan, the Great Prince. His sons raided Europe and his grandson, Kublai Khan, conquered China. The Mongols were weakened by quarrels and resistance. Later, a chief called Tamerlane* conquered an empire of his own and invaded India.

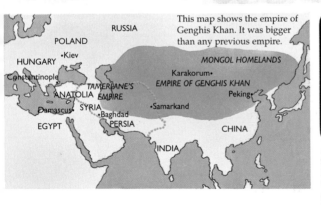

Muslim city being destroyed by Mongol raiders.

Mongols fought on horseback, using lances or bows and arrows.

Mongol commander. The Mongol army was very well-disciplined and could travel vast distances very quickly.

This shows the Mongols are moving off after destroying an enemy city. The Mongols were very cruel to their enemies. Millions of people were killed or made slaves.

This map shows the empire of Genghis Khan. It was bigger than any previous empire.

RUSSIA
POLAND
HUNGARY • Kiev
Constantinople
ANATOLIA TAMERLANE'S EMPIRE
Damascus SYRIA
EGYPT
• Baghdad PERSIA
MONGOL HOMELANDS
Karakorum •
EMPIRE OF GENGHIS KHAN
Peking
• Samarkand
CHINA
INDIA

A friar visits the Mongols

A Christian friar, was sent by St Louis of France to visit the Mongols. The Mongols had their own gods, but several of their princes had married Christian princesses.

The yurts (tents) were packed up and put on horses.

Slaves

Chief's tent was carried by ox-drawn cart.

Key dates

AD1206/1227	**Genghis Khan** ruled.
AD1240/1241	Mongols invaded Russia, Hungary and Poland.
AD1251/1259	**Mongka** was Great Khan.
AD1253/1254	Journey of **William of Rubruck**.
AD1258/1260	Baghdad and Damascus sacked by Mongols.
AD1260	Mongols defeated by the Egyptians.
AD1257/1294	**Kublai Khan** ruled China.
AD1336/1405	**Tamerlane** ruled.
AD1398	**Tamerlane** invaded north India.
AD1402	Mongols defeated the Turks.

Genghis Khan organized his empire very efficiently. He drew up a clear law code called the Yasa, encouraged trade, punished bandits and started a messenger service.

Some Mongols settled in the newly conquered lands and built cities. Others continued to live as normal in tents. There are Mongols who still live this way today.

The Christians thought that the Mongols would help them to fight the Muslims, but this never happened.

Tamerlane

1. This is the Mongol chief Timur the Lame, known in Europe as Tamerlane. He ruled his empire from the city of Samarkand.

2. This is the building in Samarkand where Tamerlane was buried. Russian archaeologists have opened his tomb.

3. By using modern methods, scientists built up a face on Tamerlane's skull, so that we now know what he looked like.

Princes and temples

India was divided into kingdoms ruled by wealthy princes. They built luxurious palaces and kept musicians and dancers to entertain them.

Indian villages worked hard to keep their fields watered for growing rice. Each village was run by a headman who carried out the orders of the local ruler.

Indians did most of their trade with Arabs. They sold silks, ivory, pearls, spices and perfumes and bought Arab horses, which could run fast.

Many people had accepted the teachings of Buddha. Pilgrims, like this Chinese monk, travelled a long way to visit sacred Buddhist shrines.

Shiva

The ancient Hindu faith became popular again. There were many gods and goddesses but the god Shiva, was one of the most important ones.

River Ganges

Hindus believe that all rivers come from the gods. The river Ganges is especially holy. For thousands of years they have bathed in it to wash away sins.

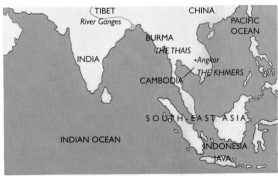

Indian religions, ideas and ways of life spread to other countries, especially in South-East Asia.

Buddhist temple in Java.

Angkor

Cambodia was one of the countries influenced by Indian ideas. In the ninth century, a people called the Khmers rose to power there. They worshipped their own kings as gods on Earth, but also worshipped Hindu gods and built huge temples, like this one at Angkor. In AD1431, a people called the Thais invaded Cambodia. The cities and temples of the Khmers were abandoned and the jungle grew up and covered them.

In AD1296, a Chinese visitor to Cambodia saw a procession like this and wrote an account of it.

Pictures, cut into the stone of Angkor, describe the battles, on land and rivers, fought by Khmers against the Chams and the Thais.

The stone carvings at Angkor display the everyday life of the Khmers. This shows men getting ready to watch two cockerels fight.

117

Silk and spice traders

In AD589, a new dynasty (family line) of emperors, called the Sui, began to rule China. They brought peace to the country after a time of long and difficult wars between rival Chinese groups.

Civil servants helped the Emperor to rule. They had to take the exams before they were given jobs in government. In the countryside, the nobles who owned most of the land, gradually became more powerful.

Peking•

Japan

CHINA

Canton•

1. Buddhism had spread from India in the 1st century AD and was very popular. But many people still believed in the teachings of Confucius and the Taoist religion. At times, Buddhists were persecuted.

A trading city in China

Some merchants travelled by sea to Africa and the Middle East.

Chinese inventions

The Chinese invented several things that were unknown to the rest of the world at this time.

They discovered how to make porcelain, a very hard, fine type of china.

At this time, the Chinese were using compasses to find their way across land and sea. This one is made of lacquered wood.

By the tenth century they used wooden blocks to print books. This is a copy of probably the oldest printed page in the world.

Gunpowder was first used for fireworks. By the 13th century, the Chinese were also using it for bombs and other weapons.

Key dates

AD589/618	Sui dynasty ruled.
AD618/906	T'ang Dynasty ruled. Buddhism very popular.
AD960/1279	Sung Dynasty ruled. Growth of trade. Mongols started attacking northern frontier.
AD1279/1368	Mongols ruled China.
AD1276/1292	**Marco Polo's** trip to China.
AD1368	Mongol rulers overthrown.
AD1368/1644	Ming Dynasty ruled.

2. Chinese craftsmen were very skillful. At the time of the T'ang emperors (AD618-906) they made fine pottery figures of animals and servants. These were placed in tombs.

3. In AD1279, the Mongols, led by the great Kublai Khan, overran China, which they then ruled for nearly 100 years.

Silk, porcelain (fine china) and carved jade were taken to the west and traded for silver and gold. Many cities grew rich because of this trade.

This caravan of camels is setting out with goods destined for the Middle East.

Marco Polo

Many foreign merchants, especially Arabs, came to China to trade. Later, adventurous Europeans arrived. Two of the European merchants who visited China were the brothers, Nicolo and Maffeo Polo, from Venice. On their second visit they took Nicolo's young son, Marco. In this picture, they are meeting Kublai Khan, the Mongol emperor of China.

Marco Polo travelled around Kublai Khan's empire for nearly 17 years. When he returned home, he wrote a book about his travels. This is the first page of his book.

Land of the Samurai

Japan is a group of islands off the coast of China. Little is known about its early history because the Japanese had no writing until it was introduced from China in the fifth century AD. The Buddhist religion also came from China, although Japan's ancient religion, Shinto, was still popular. Japanese arts, crafts, laws, taxes and the organisation of government also came from China.

SEA OF JAPAN

JAPAN

•Heian
(now Kyoto)

PACIFIC OCEAN

This is part of the Imperial city, Heian, later called Kyoto. The Emperor was at the centre of power, but noble clans (families) gradually took over and ruled for him. Many emperors retired to Buddhist monasteries. As "Cloistered Ex-Emperors", some re-established their power.

Legally all the land in Japan was owned by the Emperor. He allowed farmers, like these, to use it in return for taxes and services. Later, the nobles began to acquire their own private lands because the Emperor was not strong enough to stop them. Many battles were fought about the possession of land, and nobles gave it to their supporters as rewards.

This is Yoritomo, military leader and the chief of the Minamoto clan. In AD1192, he began to use the title "Shogun". This became the name for the head of government.

Poetry

Poetry was popular especially among the people at court. People made trips to look at the cherry blossom and see the maple leaves turning red. This inspired them to recite and write poems. There were several famous women poets.

Novels

The Japanese liked novels. This is Murasaki Shikibu, a court lady who wrote a famous novel called *The Tale of Genji*.

Armour making

Japanese warriors wore suits of armour made of tough leather strips. This is an armourer's shop where suits were made.

Helmets were made to look like the face of the wearer.

Armour made from tough leather strips

Curved swords made by highly-skilled swordsmiths

The Mongol Invasion Scroll

This scroll tells how the Mongol ruler of China, Kublai Khan, twice tried to invade Japan, but was driven back by the Samurai, and storms called the Kamikaze.

Japanese warriors were called Samurai. They fought for the nobles and had to be loyal to them. The Samurai fought hand-to-hand battles, skilfully wielding deadly two-handed swords. Before attacking, each Samurai would shout his own name and tell of the bravery of his ancestors, hoping to strike fear into the heart of his enemy.

Key dates

AD538	Buddhist religion introduced to Japan.
AD794	Capital city moved from Nara to Heian (now called Kyoto).
AD794/1185	Period of Japanese history called Heian.
AD851/1115	Fujiwara clan controlled government
AD1115/1160	Some power taken by "Cloistered Ex-Emperors".
AD1180/1185	Taira and Minamoto clans fought for control of government.
AD1185/1333	Period of Japanese history called Kamakura.
AD1274/1281	Mongol invasions.
AD1333/1336	Period of rule by the emperor.
AD1392/1573	Period of Japanese history called Ashikaga.

121

Kingdoms, traders and tribes

In AD639, Arabs, inspired by their new religion, Islam, invaded Egypt and then North Africa. They traded with the local people and brought new wealth to the area.

South of the Sahara, the land was often difficult to clear and live in. There were also dangerous diseases there. As people learnt how to make strong tools from iron, tribes were able to progress further south, clearing and farming the land as they went.

West African kingdoms

Arab traders began to make regular journeys across the Sahara. They brought gold and salt from West Africa and sold it in busy Mediterranean ports.

MEDITERRANEAN SEA

MOROCCO

EG

THE SAHARA

A great civilisatio once exi in Egypt

•Timbuktu

KINGDOM OF MALI

River Niger

AFRIC

River Congo

■ MUSLIM EMPIRE

ATLANTIC OCEAN

KALAHA DESERT

Trade made the local Africans very rich. They built magnificent cities full of palaces and mosques. The most famous city was Timbuktu, shown in this picture.

African king

Arab visitors

Some of the West African rulers had large kingdoms. One of the most important was Mali. Several Arabs who travelled to these kingdoms kept records of their visits. They were very impressed by the luxury they found, especially at court. Here, some Arabs are meeting an African king.

Portuguese explorers

From AD1420, Prince Henry of Portugal, known as "the Navigator", organized expeditions to the West African coast to trade with the Africans.

Church in Ethiopia

This picture shows a Christian church in Ethiopia. In the north, only Ethiopia managed to withstand the Muslim invasion and to keep its Christian faith.

Life in the south

In the south, different tribes adopted different ways of life.

1. In the Kalahari Desert, the Bushmen hunted animals for their food.

2. Pygmies lived in tropical jungles, hunting animals and gathering berries and fruits.

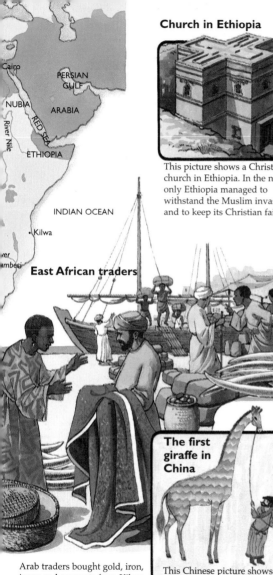

Cairo

PERSIAN GULF

NUBIA

ARABIA

RED SEA

River Nile

ETHIOPIA

INDIAN OCEAN

Kilwa

ver

mbesi

East African traders

Arab traders bought gold, iron, ivory and coconuts from Kilwa and other east coast towns, and shipped them to India and China in fast dhows (ships).

The first giraffe in China

This Chinese picture shows a giraffe arriving in China from Africa, in AD1415.

3. Tribes living in the open plains of the east and south kept animals and farmed the land.

4. People who knew how to make iron tools were very useful to their tribes.

Life in North and South America

At this time there were many separate groups of people living in different parts of the huge continent of America. In the forests, mountains, plains, deserts and jungles and in the frozen north, people found ways of surviving by hunting, fishing, gathering, and later farming. The people of North America did not have a system of writing, but archaeologists have found the remains of their settlements, which tell us something about their lives.

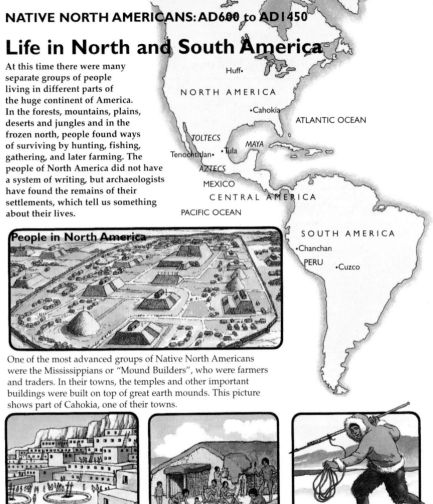

NORTH AMERICA

Huff•

•Cahokia

ATLANTIC OCEAN

TOLTECS

MAYA

Tenochtitlan• •Tula

AZTECS

MEXICO

CENTRAL AMERICA

PACIFIC OCEAN

SOUTH AMERICA

•Chanchan

PERU

•Cuzco

People in North America

One of the most advanced groups of Native North Americans were the Mississippians or "Mound Builders", who were farmers and traders. In their towns, the temples and other important buildings were built on top of great earth mounds. This picture shows part of Cahokia, one of their towns.

Some farmers lived in "pueblos", towns made of stone and mud. The houses were sometimes as high as five floors and were built in canyon walls.

At Huff, on the plain, traces of a village of more than 100 wooden houses, like this, have been found. The village was surrounded by a ditch and palisade (wooden fence).

Eskimos learnt how to live in the intense cold of the far north. They hunted caribou, seals and whales. They also fished and trapped birds.

124

Mountain farmers in Peru

What the Indians made

The people in Peru were skilled potters, weavers and metal-workers. Some of the cloth they made has lasted to the present day and is still brightly coloured.

Towns

At first, the people of Peru had small settlements. Later, they built great monuments and cities, such as the Chimu peoples' capital of Chanchan, shown above.

The first American farmers we know about, lived in the area that is now Peru. They grew maize, vegetables, cotton, tobacco and a drug called coca. Later they built terraces on the mountainside, so that they could grow crops, even on the steep slopes of the Andes. Alpacas and llamas provided wool and carried heavy loads.

The Incas

These men are Inca warriors. The Incas were a tribe who lived in the mountains of Peru. The first Inca ruler probably lived about AD1200.

In 1483, a man called Pachacutec became their king and they spread out from the city of Cuzco, their capital, to conquer a huge empire.

Key dates

North America
AD500/1500   The Mound Builders or Mississippians lived.
AD1400/1600   People living at Huff.

South America
AD200/900   Period of Peruvian civilisation called the "Classic Period".
AD1100/1438   Chimu people living at Chanchan.
AD1200   **Manco Capac** ruled the Incas.
AD1438/1471   **Pachacutec** ruled the Incas.

Central America
700BC/AD900   Maya living in Yucatan.
100BC   Zapotecs living on the south coast.
AD750/990   The Toltec Empire.
AD1325   Aztecs known to be at Tenochtitlan.

125

The Aztecs

Aztec Numbers

The Aztecs had a system of numbers, which meant they could count and keep records of their possessions. These are some of the symbols they used.

One of the earliest and greatest peoples of Central America were the Maya. This picture shows a procession of Mayan musicians.

Archaeologists have recently discovered, in the same area, more about a people called the Toltecs. This is a temple in Tula, their capital.

This is an Aztec warrior. The Aztecs probably came from western Mexico, then settled at Tenochtitlan and conquered all the land around it.

The market place

Dogs, fattened ready to be eaten.

Avocados

Tomatoes

Corn

Limes

Calendar

"New Fire Ceremony"

There was a "New Fire Ceremony" at the start of every 52 year cycle.

Schools

Children were taught by their parents. At 15, boys went to school. Schools trained priests too.

Trading was an important part of Aztec life. They had no money so they exchanged goods for others of equal value. This is called barter. Chocolate was popular, so cocoa beans were in demand, and were used for making payments. Jade and turquoise were more valuable than gold or silver.

The city of Tenochtitlan

This is the capital city of the Aztecs. It was built on islands in the middle of a lake. The lake no longer exists and modern Mexico City is built on top of it.

The Aztecs worshipped many gods and goddesses. They built temples where they killed human beings and ripped out their hearts, in order to please their gods.

Human sacrifice

Lake

Temple of Rain God

Temple of War God (Chief Aztec god)

Emperor's palace

Temple of the Feathered Serpent, one of the Aztec gods

Aztecs playing "tlachtli", a game using a rubber ball

Mosaic and feathers

Aztec craftsmen produced beautiful mosaic work, covered with small pieces of precious turquoise.

Shields, like this one, were made of feathers. The Aztecs also used feathers for making head-dresses and cloaks.

How we know

The Aztecs used picture-writing. It had not developed far enough to record complicated ideas but some religious teachings and history were recorded, and have survived in books, like this one. A book like this is called a codex.

127

The Slav people

Many of the people who now live in Eastern Europe and Western Russia are Slavs. They settled in these places in the 700s, after centuries of wandering across Europe. In the west, the Slav people set up several kingdoms for themselves. In the south, they were ruled by a people called Bulgars. In the east, the Slav people settled with the Vikings, who called the area "Rus" and so gave the name "Russia".

This map shows the Slav kingdoms during the 800s.

Some Slav kingdoms became very great and wealthy, but did not last long. One of these was Moravia. This silver plaque is one of the few Moravian things to survive.

Southern and Eastern Slavs were converted to Christianity by Byzantine missionaries. This led them to copy the Byzantine art style, as in this picture.

Boleslav I, Polish king

Western Slavs (present-day Poles and Czechs) became Christians, but joined the Roman Catholic instead of the Byzantine Church.

Some Russian states became wealthy and powerful. European kings began to take an interest in them. The most important was Kiev.

At the beginning of the 13th century, Russia was invaded by a group of Mongols called the Tartars. They destroyed many cities and made others pay them tributes, including this small town of Moscow.

Alexander Nevsky is still remembered as a hero.

One Russian prince, Alexander Nevsky, fought a battle against the Tartars to save his city, Novgorod.

Kings, Popes and princes

Florence was the capital city of one of the greatest states in Italy. In the 15th century, Florence was one of the great banking centres of Europe and was also famous as a clothmaking centre. The ruling family of Florence was called the Medici.

The Medici were very wealthy and spent a lot of money buying paintings and sculptures, and having magnificent buildings constructed, which you can still see if you visit Florence. The most brilliant of the Medici princes was Lorenzo the Magnificent.

This scene shows a procession in Florence.

In the 15th century, Italy was a collection of separate states. The central area around Rome was ruled by the Pope. Here the Pope is receiving a messenger from a foreign prince.

The Italian states were always fighting each other. In 1494, the French joined the fighting and soon the Spaniards and the emperor of the German states joined as well.

Venice was one of the wealthiest states in Italy. Its ruler was called the "Doge". This is a portrait of one of the Doges, wearing the special Doges' hat.

Art and learning

At the end of the 15th century, people in Europe began to take a great interest in art and learning, and to develop new ideas about the world. They started asking questions and doing experiments instead of just accepting existing ideas. People began to think that civilisation had been at its best in Ancient Greece and Rome, so they revived Greek and Roman ideas. The time became known as the "Renaissance", which means revival or rebirth. It began in Italy and gradually spread across Europe.

In the Renaissance, Italians began to be interested in the remains of Ancient Rome. They dug up statues and other treasures and made collections of them.

This is the city of Florence in Italy. The new ideas of the Renaissance began here and many of the most famous men of this time lived and worked in Florence.

Painting

1. Before the Renaissance, artists painted mainly religious scenes. Their pictures looked flat and the people they painted did not look very lifelike.

2. In the late 14th and early 15th centuries, painters tried to make the people in their paintings look as lifelike as possible.

3. Besides painting religious subjects, Renaissance painters did pictures of everyday life and stories from Ancient Greece and Rome.

Sculpture

4. Artists began to use live models to help them paint lifelike people. This is Simonetta Vespucci, who modelled for the artist Botticelli.

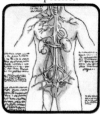

5. Artists studied nature and the human body to help them draw things more accurately. This sketch is from Leonardo da Vinci's notebook.

6. Artists learned how to show distance in their paintings, making you feel you could walk into them. This is called "perspective".

Sculptors were inspired by the statues of Ancient Greece and Rome. This marble statue was made by Michelangelo. He was also a painter, an architect and a poet.

1. Many new schools and universities were founded. The main subjects were Greek and Latin grammar. In England the new schools were called "grammar" schools.

2. Scholars studied texts in Greek, Latin and Hebrew. They were excited by the thoughts and ideas of ancient times. The invention of printing helped to spread these ideas.

3. Studying ancient Christian texts made some people, like Erasmus, the Dutch scholar in this picture, criticize the Church and its priests for being corrupt.

4. People also began to study politics. This is Machiavelli, an Italian, who wrote a book about politics called "The Prince", in which he said that a ruler had to be ruthless.

Architecture

Architects built wonderful palaces and churches. They used domes and copied the style of Greek and Roman temples. The towers and spires of the Middle Ages went out of fashion.

A properly educated Renaissance person was expected to be able to:

Understand and collect art, write poetry, play a musical instrument,

read and write Latin and Greek, speak several languages, fight if necessary,

take part in politics, ride and be good at sports, show good manners to everyone.

Science and inventions

The ideas of the Renaissance made people keen to question everything about the world around them. Some people began doing experiments to test their ideas.

People called "alchemists", tried to brew potions that would cure all ills, give eternal life and turn lead into gold.

One of the greatest men of the Renaissance was Leonardo da Vinci. He was a painter and an inventor. He thought a lot about making a flying machine. This is a model based on one of his designs, which he worked out by watching birds fly. Leonardo also studied animals and humans to find out how they worked. He also painted the very famous picture of the Mona Lisa.

The printing press was probably the most important invention of this time. The first one was made by a German called Johann Gutenberg. Books could now be produced quickly and cheaply, instead of having to be handwritten as before. This meant ideas and learning spread more quickly.

In England, people experimented with metals and learnt how to make cheap and reliable cannons out of cast iron. These soon replaced the expensive bronze cannons that the Germans and Italians had been making.

In the Middle Ages, the only clocks were huge ones on public buildings. The invention of springs made it possible to make watches and small clocks. Pendulum clocks were invented too.

Instruments were invented to help sailors steer their ships more accurately. To use them, a captain had to be good at mathematics and know the stars. Gradually new and better maps were made.

Medicine

In 1543, a Belgian doctor called Andreas Vesalius published a book about how the human body worked. This shows him lecturing to his students at the university in Padua. William Harvey, another great doctor, discovered and proved that the heart pumps blood round the body.

The invention of microscopes made people realize for the first time that the world was full of minute creatures, too small to see unless they are magnified.

Ideas about the universe

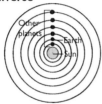

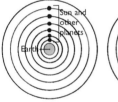

From the time of the Ancient Greeks, people had believed that the Earth was the centre of the universe and that the Sun, Moon and stars moved round it. In 1543, the Polish astronomer, Copernicus, published a book showing that the Sun, not the Earth, was the centre of the universe.

The invention of the telescope in the early 17th century meant that people could get a better view of the stars and planets. The Italian scientist, Galileo, made a telescope strong enough to show the separate stars of the Milky Way. The Catholic Church forbade him to teach his theories.

Scientific societies were founded and special places were built, like the Royal Observatory near London, to study stars.

The English scientist, Sir Isaac Newton, discovered many things, including that white light is made up of many colours.

Key dates

AD1444/1510	Italian painter **Botticelli**.
AD1452/1519	Italian artist/inventor **Leonardo da Vinci**.
AD1454	**Gutenberg** invented his printing press.
AD1466/1536	Dutch scholar **Erasmus**.
AD1469/1527	Italian writer **Machiavelli**.
AD1473/1543	Polish astronomer **Copernicus**.
AD1475/1564	Italian artist **Michelangelo**.
AD1514/1564	Belgian doctor **Vesalius**.
AD1564/1642	Italian astronomer **Galileo**.
AD1578/1657	English doctor **Harvey**.
AD1600 (approx.)	Invention of telescope and microscope.
AD1642/1727	English scientist **Newton**.

133

New ideas about religion

The people of Western Europe were all Roman Catholics, but by AD1500, many were unhappy with the way the Church was run. The Popes and many of the priests seemed interested only in wealth and power and set a bad example in the way they lived their lives. This led to a movement, which became known as the "Reformation", to change and reform the Christian Church. People who joined the movement were called "Protestants" because they were protesting about things that they thought were wrong.

1. In 1517, a German monk called Martin Luther nailed a list of 95 complaints about the Church and the way priests behaved, to the door of Wittenberg church in Germany.

2. Luther believed everyone should be able to study God's message for themselves. So he translated the Bible from Latin into German. Versions in other languages quickly followed.

3. Luther was condemned by the Church court, but some German princes supported him. He also won many followers across Europe.

4. King Henry VIII of England wanted to divorce. The Pope would not let him, so Henry made himself head of the Church of England.

John Calvin

5. Soon there were other religious leaders. Protestants split into groups. John Calvin set up a new Church in Geneva.

6. Protestants and Catholics were tortured and hanged. Both sides believed they would save their opponents from hell this way.

Catholics fight back

1. The Pope called a meeting of churchmen in Trent, Italy. They laid down Catholic beliefs and ordered obedience to them.

St Ignatius Loyola

2. St Ignatius Loyola founded the Society of Jesus. Members, called Jesuits, tried to win Protestants back to the Catholic Church.

3. Protestants disapproved of decorated churches, but Catholics introduced an even more elaborate style, called Baroque.

4. In Spain, the most fiercely Catholic country in Europe, an organization called the Inquisition hunted out anyone who was not a good Catholic. Torture was used to make people confess their beliefs. Protestants who refused to become Catholics were burnt to death at special ceremonies called "Auto-de-fe" (Spanish for "acts of faith"), which were watched by huge crowds.

Murders and executions

1. William of Orange led a revolt of Dutch Protestants against the Spanish, who ruled Holland. He was murdered by a Catholic.

2. On the eve of St Bartholomew's Day in 1572, Catholics laid a plot and murdered all the Protestants they could find in Paris.

3. Mary, Queen of Scots, a Catholic, was executed for plotting against Elizabeth I, Queen of England, a Protestant.

This map of Europe in AD1600, shows which areas were Catholic and which had become Protestant.

- Protestant
- Mixture of Catholic and Protestant
- Catholic

Key dates

AD1483/1546	Life of **Martin Luther**.
AD1517	Luther nailed 95 complaints to Wittenburg church door.
AD1534	**Henry VIII** became head of the Church of England. **Ignatius Loyola** founded the Jesuits (Society of Jesus).
AD1536	**John Calvin** began work in Geneva.
AD1545/1563	The Council of Trent.
AD1555	Fighting between Catholics and Protestants in Germany ended by treaty called Peace of Augsburg.
AD1572	The Massacre of St Bartholomew's Eve.
AD1584	**William of Orange** was assassinated.
D1587	**Mary Queen of Scots** was executed.

War and weapons

Guns were invented at the beginning of the 14th century. It was many years before they came into general use, but over the next few centuries they changed the way wars were fought. The knights and castles of the Middle Ages gradually disappeared. Their armour was no protection against bullets, and they could not get close enough to the enemy to use their swords and lances. Castle walls could not stand up to an attack of cannon balls.

1. From about 1300 onwards, archers started using longbows which were very effective against knights. They had a long range and were quite accurate.

2. Castles and walled towns had been difficult to capture, but when cannons began to be used in the 15th century, even the thickest walls could be quickly battered down.

This is a German knight charging a peasant.

3. Armour and weapons were expensive. When peasants rebelled, as they often did, they had little chance against well-armed knights and nobles.

4. When hand-guns were invented they took a long time to load. Pikemen were positioned next to the gunmen to protect them as they reloaded.

Musketeer

5. Guns called muskets were invented. They were accurate but heavy, so musketeers supported their guns on forked sticks.

6. Pistols were less accurate and fired a shorter distance. They were used by cavalry who fired at the enemy then rode away to reload.

7. Bayonets (blades which attached to the end of a gun) allowed gunmen to defend themselves at close-quarters.

8. Instead of relying on their nobles to raise armies, or hiring mercenary soldiers, kings began to set up permanent armies of their own. These armies were more highly-trained than before and could obey orders at speed. Commanders had to study hard to learn how to plan their battles and campaigns.

9. The Dutch and English developed lighter ships which could turn more quickly. This helped the English fleet to defeat the Spanish Armada.

10. On ships, cannons were placed along each side. Enemies fired "broadside" at each other so they had more chance of hitting their target.

11. Disease, bad food and harsh punishments made life at sea very hard. Governments often used "press-gangs" to kidnap men for the navy.

Key dates

AD1455/1485 Wars of the Roses: civil war in England.

AD1494/1559 Italian Wars: Italian states fighting each other. France and the Holy Empire joined in.

AD1524/1525 Peasants' War in Germany: the German peasants rebelled.

AD1562/1598 Wars of Religion in France: fighting between French Catholics and Protestants.

AD1568/1609 Dutch Revolt: the Dutch rebelled against their Spanish rulers.

AD1588 The **Spanish Armada** was defeated by the English fleet.

AD1618/1648 Thirty Years War: fought mainly in Germany. Involved most of the countries of Europe.

AD1642/1649 Civil War in England.

AD1648/1653 Wars of the "Fronde": two rebellions against the French government.

AD1652/1654 Wars between the Dutch
1665/1667 & and the English. Fought at
1672/1674 sea. Caused by rivalry over trade.

AD1701/1714 Wars of the Spanish Succession: France and Spain against England, Austria and Holland.

AD1733/1735 Wars of the Polish Succession: Austria and Russia against France and Spain about who should rule Poland.

AD1740/1748 War of the Austrian Succession: Austria, Britain and Russia against France and Prussia.

The Incas

The Incas lived in the mountains of Peru in South America. Their capital was called Cuzco. From about 1440AD, they began to conquer lands and build up a huge empire. The empire lasted about a hundred years before Spanish soldiers arrived in search of gold and conquered them.

White llamas to be sacrificed.

Temple

Atahualpa

Body of Huayna Capac

Musicians with drums, rattles and flutes.

The emperor of the Incas was called the Inca. His people thought he was descended from the Sun. When he died his body was preserved and honoured.

This is the funeral procession of an emperor called Huayna Capac. His son, Atahualpa, became the new emperor by fighting his half-brother, Huascar.

Unfortunately this war was just before the Spaniards arrived and it greatly weakened the Incas in their fight against the European invaders.

Inca priests were important people. They held services, heard confessions and foretold the future by looking into fire. The Sun was their chief god.

Women were taught how to weave and spin wool. Some, who were especially chosen for their beauty, became priestesses called the Virgins of the Sun.

The Incas were very skilled at making things out of gold. This gold glove was found in a tomb. Beside it is a model of a god, set with precious stones.

138

A farming village

Land was terraced so that crops can be grown on the steep mountainside.

Peasants dug fields with pointed sticks.

Buildings made with heavy blocks of stone were built without the help of machinery or iron tools.

Villagers ate mainly maize and vegetables.

Weaving

Guinea pigs were kept for food.

Men drank "chicha" beer.

PACIFIC OCEAN

Quito

Cuzco

INCA EMPIRE

All the land belonged to the Inca. One third of the crops was kept by peasants, who lived in mountain villages, like this one, and worked on the land. Another third went to the priests and the last third went to the Inca. With his share, he paid his officials, soldiers and craftsmen.

Keeping records

The Incas had no system of writing but their officials used "quipus" to help them record things. Coloured strings stood for objects. Knots tied in the strings stood for numbers.

Roads and messengers

A well-maintained network of roads linked all parts of the Inca empire. There were hanging bridges, made of twisted straw and vines. Peasants built and repaired roads and bridges. There were no wheeled vehicles so goods were carried by llamas.

Relays of fast runners carried messages and quipus. There were rest houses, a day's journey apart, for the runners to stay in.

The discovery of America

Until the end of the 15th century, Europeans did not know that the huge continent of America existed. Explorers and traders had made long and difficult journeys eastwards to China and India, bringing back spices, silks and jewels. These were in such demand in Europe that people thought there might be a quicker way to the Far East by sea. The Portuguese sailed to the east around Africa, but others thought it might be quicker to go westwards. When they did, they found America in their way.

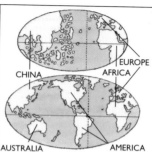

1. These two maps show the world as people in Europe thought it looked in about 1490 (top) and as it really looked (bottom).

2. An Italian, called Christopher Columbus, persuaded King Ferdinand and Queen Isabella of Spain to pay for an expedition to find China by sailing west instead of east. He set off in 1492 with three ships.

The Spanish conquerors

Spanish adventurers ("conquistadors") started to explore the mainland, hoping to find treasure. They discovered the Aztecs in Mexico and the Incas in Peru.

1. Spanish soldiers, led by Hernando Cortes, attacked the Aztecs. There were fewer of them, but the Spaniards had better weapons and soon conquered Mexico, calling it New Spain.

2. Cortes won the support of Indian tribes, who helped him to defeat the Aztecs.

3. The Inca emperor tried to buy his freedom by offering the Spanish gold, but was killed.

4. Indians who refused to become Christians were burnt to death by the Spaniards.

5. The Spaniards treated the Indians cruelly. Many were put to work in silver mines.

3. After five weeks, Columbus reached what he thought were islands off China but were, in fact, the West Indies. Later, he made three more voyages and reached the mainland of America.

4. To stop Spain and Portugal fighting about who owned the newly discovered lands, the Pope drew a line on the map. All new lands to the east of the line went to Portugal, those to the west went to Spain.

5. There were many expeditions to explore the new lands. The first to sail round South America was led by Magellan. He was killed on the way, but his ship returned and was the first to sail right round the world.

Slave trade

The Spanish and Portuguese brought Africans over as slaves. John Hawkins, an English captain, joined the trade, against their ban.

Pirates

AZTEC EMPIRE

INCA EMPIRE

Columbus' route

WEST INDIES

Pope's line

Magellan's route

French and English sea-captains were encouraged by their governments to be pirates and were rewarded for bringing back Spanish treasure.

Key dates

AD1492	First voyage of **Christopher Columbus**.
AD1494	The Pope divided the new lands between Spain and Portugal.
AD1498	**Vasco da Gama** sailed round Africa and reached India.
AD1500	**Pedro Cabral** claimed Brazil for the Portuguese government.
AD1519/1522	**Magellan's** voyage round the world.
AD1519	**Hernando Cortes** landed in Mexico.
AD1521	Fall of Aztec capital **Atahualpa**.
AD1562/1568	**John Hawkins** shipping African slaves to Spanish America.

Muslim Empires

St Sophia in Istanbul

From 1300, the Ottoman Turks, a Muslim* people, began to build an empire. In 1453, they captured Constantinople, the centre of the Orthodox Christian Church and renamed it Istanbul. Its great cathedral, St Sophia, became a mosque.

Led by Sultan, Suleiman the Magnificent, the Ottomans defeated the Hungarian army at the Battle of Mohács and took control of Hungary. They threatened Europe until 1683, when they besieged Vienna and were heavily defeated.

The Sultan's palace

Slaves

Here an Ottoman Sultan receives a European envoy in the Topkapi Saray, his palace in Istanbul. European princes were eager to make alliances with the Turks.

The Ottomans took boys from Christian areas of their empire, away from their families, and brought them up as Muslims.

Most of the boys were trained to be soldiers called Janissaries. They were the best troops in the Ottoman's army.

The cleverest of these boys were given a good education, and later they were made government officials.

EMPIRE OF SAFAVID PERSIANS

EMPIRE OF OTTOMAN TURKS

*Muslims belong to a religion called Islam.

Muslims in Persia

1. The Persians belonged to a group of Muslims called the Shi'ites. This mosque is in Isfahan, their capital city.

2. The Persians and Ottomans often fought over religion and land. Their wars lasted on and off for over 200 years.

3. The Persian royal family was called the Safavids. During the reign of their greatest shah (king), Abbas I, the luxuries of Persia became world famous.

Spain and the Muslims

1. In the eighth century, Muslims had overrun Spain, but were driven out by King Ferdinand and Queen Isabella.

2. Some Muslims stayed in Spain and became Christians, but years later their descendants were banished.

3. The Spaniards did not want the Ottomans in the Mediterranean Sea. In 1571, they defeated them at the Battle of Lepanto.

4. North African pirates raided the coasts of European countries and took people to sell as slaves in Muslim lands.

143

The Habsburgs

SPANISH HABSBURG LANDS

AUSTRIAN HABSBURG LANDS

The Habsburgs were the most powerful ruling family in Europe in the 16th century. They were rulers of Austria and in 1516, the Habsburg Archduke, Charles V, inherited Spain and the newly won Spanish territories in America too. When Charles died, his empire was divided between his son, Philip II of Spain and his brother, Ferdinand, Archduke of Austria. From then on Spain and Austria were ruled by separate branches of the Habsburg family.

•Moscow

Russian Empire at time of Peter the Great

Constantinople

1. Fabulous riches were sent to Spain from South America, but wars against the French, the Protestants and the Turks put Spanish kings in debt.

2. You can see some of the magnificent clothes which were worn at the Spanish court in the paintings of Velasquez, King Philip IV's court artist.

3. The Spanish kings were strong supporters of the Catholic Church. They encouraged the Inquisition to find and punish heretics.

Don Quixote, with his servant Sancho Panza

4. At this time there were many famous writers and artists in Spain. Miguel de Cervantes wrote a famous book called *Don Quixote*.

Holy Roman Emperors

A group of seven German princes always elected the Habsburg Archduke of Austria because the Habsburgs were so powerful. The Archduke ruled over the hundreds of German states. This was difficult as many of the German princes had become Protestant and resented having a Catholic ruler.

The Tsars

Before 1450, Russia was divided into several different states, each with its own ruler. During the 15th century, the Grand Prince of Moscow gradually gained control of all the states. The Russians belonged to the Orthodox Christian Church, which had its centre at Constantinople. But when the Turks, who were Muslims, conquered Constantinople in 1453, Moscow saw itself as the centre of the Orthodox Church.

1. Grand Prince Ivan III of Moscow was the first to use the title "Tsar" and have this double-headed eagle as his emblem.

2. Ivan III ordered that Moscow's fortress, the Kremlin, should be rebuilt. He brought Italian architects to build the cathedral, shown here, inside its walls.

3. Ivan IV (1533-1584), often known as Ivan the Terrible because of his cruelty, won great victories over the Tartars and also gained control of all the Russian nobles. He encouraged trade with Europe and in this picture, receives envoys from Elizabeth I of England.

4. When Ivan the Terrible died, the nobles fought for power until a national assembly chose Michael Romanov, shown in this picture, to be the Tsar.

Peter the Great

Peter the Great (1689-1725) wanted Russia to be a powerful modern state. He made nobles cut off their beards to look more European.

Peter went to Holland and England to learn about ship-building. He brought European craftsmen back with him to build him a navy.

In 1709, Peter led the Russians to a great victory over Sweden, their main rival, at the Battle of Poltava.

Peter wanted Russia to have the grandest capital city in Europe, so he built St Petersburg on the edge of the Baltic Sea.

The Elizabethans

From 1485 to 1603, England was ruled by a family called the Tudors. The best-known of the Tudor rulers are Henry VIII, who separated the English Church from the Roman Catholic Church, and his daughter, Elizabeth I. When Elizabeth was only three, her mother, Anne Boleyn, was executed. During the reigns of her half-brother Edward VI and half-sister, Mary, Elizabeth's life was often in danger, but she survived to become one of England's most brilliant rulers.

1. This is a painting of Elizabeth. She reigned for 45 years, keeping a magnificent court where she inspired writers, artists and explorers. She never married.

2. This is a Protestant preacher. Elizabeth declared that the Church of England was Protestant, but she did not persecute people who had other beliefs unless they plotted against her.

Explorers

This is Sir Walter Raleigh. He introduced tobacco and potatoes to England from America.

Explorers tried to sail north to reach the Far East. They all failed because they could not sail through the ice.

Merchants banded together to form companies to trade overseas, licensed by the government.

The Globe Theatre

The more expensive seats were in the galleries.

Pit where poorer people and apprentices stood

The theatre was built of wood with a thatched roof so there was always a danger of fire. (It did, in fact, burn down in 1613, but has now been rebuilt.)

Francis Drake

Francis Drake led attacks on Spanish ships and colonies and captured treasure from them. Elizabeth had him knighted on his ship, the Golden Hinde, after he had sailed round the world. When the Spaniards sent an Armada (fleet) to invade England, Drake played a leading part in their defeat.

3. By avoiding expensive wars, Elizabeth helped England become very wealthy. The nobles and middle classes spent their money on splendid houses, furniture and clothes.

4. Beggars and thieves were a terrible problem. A new law was made which said that all districts must provide work for the poor and shelter those who could not work.

Portraits

We know what many famous Elizabethans looked like from the miniature portraits by an artist called Nicholas Hilliard. This is a picture he painted of himself.

Musicians

Several great musicians lived at this time. Two of the most famous were Thomas Tallis and William Byrd. They composed music to be played at home, as well as a great deal of church music.

The trumpeter blew a fanfare when the play was about to begin.

The flag showed that a play was being performed.

Inner stage can be curtained off for indoor scenes.

There were no professional actresses so boys took women's parts.

The Globe in London was the most famous theatre built at this time. Before theatres, plays were performed in inn courtyards and town squares.

Shakespeare was an actor and writer with one of the London companies. He wrote at least 36 plays. Many of them were first performed at the Globe theatre.

147

European settlers

An Native North American village

Land cleared by burning

Boys fishing

Chief

Long houses made of bark

Party of hunters bringing a deer home

Palisade made of tree trunks

Ritual dance

When the first Europeans arrived in North America, there were hundreds of tribes of native people there. Each had their own customs, language and way of life. On the east coast, they lived in villages and hunted and farmed for food. This picture is based on drawings made by early European settlers. The arrival of Europeans in the early 17th century was a disaster for Native North Americans. Many died of diseases brought from Europe and many others were killed or driven from their lands.

13 colonies

This map shows the 13 colonies where the Europeans settled.

1. In 1607, English settlers set up a colony at Jamestown. This shows their leader, Captain John Smith, being rescued from death by Pocahontas, the daughter of a local Native North American chief.

2. In 1620, some English people known as the Pilgrim Fathers sailed to America in the ship, the "Mayflower". They were Puritans, who wanted freedom to worship God their own way.

3. Puritans called the area where they settled New England. During their first winter they struggled to get food.

4. Native North Americans helped the English to survive. After their first harvest they held a feast to thank God. "Thanksgiving Day" is still celebrated.

5. Many Europeans sailed to live in America. This picture shows a ship full of settlers unloading. Some went because they wanted religious freedom, some were escaping from troubles at home and others went hoping to find adventure, or a better life and land of their own. Settlers on the east coast formed 13 colonies, each with their own laws and system of government. Gradually they were all brought under the control of the British government.

6. Most settlers were farmers. Native North Americans were hostile, so it was hard work defending themselves.

7. In the south, settlers grew tobacco and got rich as there was a craze for it in Europe. African slaves worked for them.

Part of 18th century Boston

8. Trade with Europe became profitable and some of the money was used to build large towns.

9. Some people, mainly French, lived as trappers and hunters and explored the Mississippi River.

Plantations and trading forts

West Indies

From the 1620s, most of the West Indies were taken over by the French and English, who set up sugar plantations. Slaves from Africa worked for them.

Fierce pirates infested the Caribbean Sea at this time. One English pirate called Henry Morgan was eventually knighted by King Charles II.

Key dates

AD1497	**John Cabot** discovered Newfoundland.
AD1523	French begin to explore Canada.
AD1607	English colony set up in Virginia.
AD1608	French founded the settlement of Quebec.
AD1612	First English colony in West Indies set up on Bermuda.
AD1655	English captured Jamaica from Spaniards.
AD1682	The French set up settlements in Louisiana.
AD1759	**General James Wolfe** captured Quebec from the French.
AD1763	Treaty of Paris. England took over Canada from the French.

Canada

Many French and English people settled in Canada. Some were farmers. Many trapped animals for fur and caught and salted fish. They bought supplies at forts set up by trading companies. The fish and furs were then sent to Europe.

The capture of Quebec

The lands belonging to England's Hudson Bay Company in Canada and the 13 colonies in America were separated from the French colonies in Canada. From the 1680s, rivalry between the French and British grew and fighting broke out. Here, British troops, led by general Wolfe, are reaching the top of the cliffs above the St Lawrence River before making a surprise attack on the French city of Quebec. After the capture of Quebec, the English gained control of all of Canada.

150

The Kingdom of Benin

1. Today, Benin is a small country in West Africa, but between AD1450 and AD1850 it was the capital city of a great kingdom. European explorers brought back reports that Benin's warriors were highly disciplined and very brave, and were constantly fighting to win more land and slaves.

2. The people of Benin had no system of writing, but they made bronze plaques to record important events. This plaque shows their king, who was called the Oba, sacrificing a cow. The Obas spent most of their time in religious ceremonies and let their counsellors govern.

3. The Portuguese were the first Europeans to explore the coast of Africa. Soon others came, to buy ivory, gold and especially slaves sold by the local chiefs.

4. The most promising boys were trained as hunters. If they were good they could become elephant hunters, armed with blow-guns and poisonous darts.

5. Benin lost its power in the 19th century, but the people still survive. This present-day chief is dressed for a festival in honour of the Oba's father.

Music

Benin musicians played bells and elephant-tusk trumpets. This carving shows a drummer.

Carvings

The people of Benin made beautiful portrait heads, like this one of a queen mother.

There were many skilled craftsmen in Benin. They made things from ivory.

Ivory bracelets

PORTUGAL

Route of Portuguese traders

Slaves to America

BENIN

The Mogul Empire

Muslim warriors had been invading and setting up kingdoms in India since before the 10th century. The most famous Muslim invaders were the Moguls, who were descended from the Mongols. In 1526, they founded the great Mogul Empire in north-west India which lasted until 1858. During their rule, great progress was made in the arts and sciences. Most Indians continued to work on the land, however, as their ancestors had done for centuries before them.

1. This is the first Mogul emperor, Babur (1526-1530). He was a descendant of the Mongol chiefs, Tamerlane and Genghis Khan.

2. This is the court of Babur's grandson, Akbar (1556-1605), greatest of the Mogul emperors. He was a good soldier and a wise ruler. He encouraged artists and brought scholars to try to find one religion.

3. Moguls were influenced by Persian art and learning. This is Akbar's son, whose wife is Persian. Her name, Nurjahan, meant "Light of the World".

4. Moguls built many wonderful buildings. The most famous is the Taj Mahal. It was built by Emperor Shah Jahan, as a tomb for his wife Mumtaz Mahal.

5. Mogul emperors and nobles enjoyed hunting. Sometimes they used cheetahs for hunting gazelle. They hunted tigers while riding on the backs of elephants.

6. European merchants came to India to buy silks, cotton, ivory, dyes and spices, and set up trading posts across India.

Mogul prince preparing for battle

7. As the power of Mogul rulers grew weaker, the British and French used the rivalry of lesser princes to increase their own power.

THE MOGUL EMPIRE

• BRITISH AND FRENCH TRADING POSTS

Ming and Ch'ing Emperors

The emperors of China lived in Peking, in a fantastic palace called the "Forbidden City". This picture shows the richly decorated buildings and lovely gardens which surrounded the palace. The Ming dynasty – family line – of emperors (AD1368/1644) cut themselves off from the government and let their officials rule for them. In AD1644, the last Ming emperor committed suicide and the Ch'ing dynasty won power. They ruled until AD1911. Many of the Ch'ing emperors were clever rulers and brought peace and prosperity to China.

This figure, carved in ivory, represents a public official. To obtain this job he had to take a series of difficult exams.

Chinese doctors boiled herbs to make medicines. They treated patients by sticking needles in them (acupuncture).

This is a scene from *The Water Margin*, one of China's few novels. It tells a story of bandits protecting the poor.

Missionaries from Europe, like these Jesuit priests were welcomed by emperors at first, but were later driven out.

Porcelain
Silk
Jade
Lacquer
Tea

Europeans wanted beautiful Chinese goods, but had to pay in gold and silver because China did not want European goods.

Farming

New crops, such as maize, were introduced from America by Portuguese and Spanish traders. During the period of peace under the Ch'ing emperors the population increased. Gradually, it became difficult to grow enough to feed everyone.

153

Life in Japan

The emperors of Japan were greatly honoured, but had no real power. The country was ruled by an official called the Shogun. The first Europeans reached Japan in the 1540s and for nearly a century they traded with the Japanese. But then the Shogun expelled all foreign merchants, except the Chinese and the Dutch, and the Japanese people remained totally cut off from the rest of the world until 1854.

In 1467, civil war broke out. For over 100 years, local barons, called daimyos, fought each other. They built huge castles, like this one, half-fortress, half-palace, where they lived with their warriors, the samurai. The samurai were very loyal to their daimyo. Eventually, a powerful daimyo called Tokugawa Ieyasu, succeeded in uniting Japan. He became Shogun and ruled from his capital in Edo (now Tokyo). The Tokugawa family held power until 1868.

The ancient Japanese Shinto faith was popular in the 18th century. This is a baby being taken into a Shinto shrine.

Tea drinking became an elaborate ceremony, which still plays a part in Japanese life. Both the ceremony and the tea were originally brought from China by Buddhist monks. The tea is prepared, served and drunk according to strict rules.

Jesuits brought Christianity to Japan. Many people converted, but later, Shoguns executed Christians.

Arranging flowers was a special art, called Ikebana, which at first only men were allowed to do. Different flowers and arrangements had special meanings.

Pictures made by printing from carved blocks of wood became popular at this time. Most of them illustrate the lives of ordinary people.

This is a street bookseller in the 18th century. Poetry and novels were popular, but there were no longer many women writers, as there had been earlier.

Puppet theatres and musical plays called "Kabuki" became very popular. These were livelier and more realistic than older Japanese dramas.

A Dutch island

From 1630, Dutch merchants lived on this island in Nagasaki Bay. They were not expelled like other foreigners because the Shoguns felt they would not try to conquer or convert the Japanese. A bridge linked the island to the land, but the Dutch were not allowed to cross it.

Key dates

AD1467/1568 Period of civilisation in Japan.
AD1543 First Portuguese traders reached Japan. Other Europeans follow.
AD1549/1551 St Xavier working in Japan.
AD1592&1597 Japanese invaded Korea.
AD1600/1868 Tokugawa family rule.
AD1603 **Tokugawa Ieyasu** became Shogun.
AD1606/1630 Christians persecuted.
AD1623/1639 All Europeans, except a few Dutch, left Japan.

Merchants and trade

Once explorers had discovered new lands and sea-routes in the 16th century, there was a huge increase in trade between Europe and the rest of the world. By the 17th century, the main trading countries were Holland, England and France. In these countries, the merchants and middle classes who organized this trade became very wealthy and began to copy the lifestyle of the nobles. Even some of the ordinary working people benefited from this increase in wealth.

Groups of merchants, like these, set up trading companies in which people could buy shares. The shareholders' money was used to pay the cost of trading ventures. Any profit was divided amongst the shareholders.

Many merchants bought goods from people who worked in their own homes and sold them abroad. In this picture, a merchant's agent is buying cloth from a family workshop.

Countries competing for overseas trade had to have good ships, sailors and ports. Dutch ships were among the best.

Rich merchants began to set up banks to lend money. For this service, they charged a fee called "interest". People could also bring their money to the bank for safe-keeping. In the 17th century, London and Amsterdam became the most important banking cities.

In big European cities, people met to buy and sell shares and discuss business in coffee houses.

It soon became more convenient to have a proper building for use as a market where people could buy and sell shares. This is the Amsterdam Stock Exchange, built in 1613.

Merchants paid a fee to insurance companies, who stood the cost of disastrous expeditions.

As merchant classes grew rich, they built big town houses. Fashionable areas had pavements and wide streets.

The new middle classes wanted to live like the nobles. Many of them became rich enough to buy country estates and obtained titles. Some of the nobility looked down on them but others were happy to marry into these wealthy families.

Governments needed to understand business and finance so some merchants were chosen as royal ministers and advisers.

We know what some Dutch merchants of this time looked like because many of them paid artists to paint their portraits.

Many paintings of this time, especially Dutch ones, show how merchant families lived and what their homes looked like.

In every country, there were still many desperately poor people. Some nobles and merchants tried to help the poor. They founded hospitals, homes for old people and orphanages. Here a group of merchants' wives are inspecting an orphanage run by nuns.

Dutch merchants find Australia

On their trips to the east, Dutch sailors discovered Australia, which they called New Holland. Their early attempts to settle there failed.

The Dutch controlled most of the important spice trade between Europe and the East Indies. This made Holland the greatest trading nation in Europe for much of the 17th century. This map shows the Dutch empire in the East Indies and the things they went there to buy.

EAST INDIES

AUSTRALIA

- ● Dutch bases
- △ Rice
- ■ Pepper
- ○ Sugar
- ▲ Cloves
- ✥ Nutmeg
- ◈ Ivory
- ✦ Diamonds
- ☉ Tin
- ✳ Precious woods

Kings and parliaments

1. In the 17th and 18th centuries, much of Europe was ruled by extremely powerful kings, queens and emperors. These rulers are known as "absolute monarchs".

The court of Louis XIV of France was the most brilliant in Europe. This is the Hall of Mirrors in his palace at Versailles. He encouraged the French nobles to come and live at his court and be entertained, so that he could keep an eye on them. Other monarchs built themselves great palaces too and tried to imitate Louis' way of life.

The English parliament

Parliament supporter
("Roundhead")

King's
supporter ("Cavalier")

1. King Charles I of England tried to ignore parliament and rule like an absolute monarch. Many people were so unhappy with the way he ruled that in 1642 civil war broke out.

2. The king was defeated and executed. Oliver Cromwell, the leader of the parliamentarian army became ruler. He could not get parliament to agree with him so also tried to rule without them.

3. Oliver Cromwell died in 1658. His son was incompetent and no one would support his government. Eventually Charles I's son was invited back and crowned King Charles II.

2. Parliaments hardly ever met. The king made all the important decisions. His ministers could only advise him. In order to keep control, a successful ruler, like Louis XIV, spent hours every day with his ministers in meetings like this one.

Madame de Pompadour

3. Sometimes the king's favourites became very powerful. Louis XV let Madame du Pompadour make decisions.

4. The king made the laws and could put his enemies in prison if he wanted. Law-courts did what the king wanted.

5. Absolute monarchs usually kept permanent armies. Frederick the Great of Prussia, which is now part of Germany, was a brilliant military commander. Here he is inspecting his troops.

6. Mozart played the piano in Maria Teresa's court. Monarchs invited writers and painters, too.

Glasswork

7. To add to their strength, rulers set up industries, producing luxury goods such as silk and glass.

4. Parliament's power increased, however, and the king's minister had to have the support of its members. This is Robert Walpole, one of the most successful ministers of the 18th century.

5. Members of parliament formed two political parties called the Whigs and the Tories. Only people who owned property worth more than a certain value could vote.

Key dates

AD1642	English Civil War began.
AD1643/1715	**Louis XIV** ruled France.
AD1649	**Charles I** was executed.
AD1658	**Oliver Cromwell** died.
AD1660/1685	Reign of **Charles II**.
AD1682/1725	**Peter the Great** ruled Russia.
AD1715/1774	**Louis XV** ruled France.
AD1730/1741	**Robert Walpole** was Prime Minister.
AD1740/1780	**Maria Teresa** ruled Austria.
AD1740/1786	**Frederick the Great** ruled Prussia (now part of Germany).
AD1756/1791	Life of **Mozart**.
AD1762/1796	**Catherine the Great** ruled Russia.

Sports and pastimes

Nobles and kings played an early version of tennis on special courts. Bowls was also a favourite game at this time.

Cock-fighting was a popular sport. Cockerels were specially trained to fight, often to the death.

Fox-hunting was a sport for the wealthy. Horse-racing, introduced later on, interested a wider audience.

All classes of people watched bear or bull baiting. The animal was put in a ring and fierce dogs set onto it to kill it.

The English village of Hambledon had the first recognized cricket club. The game was later introduced to many of the countries in the British Empire.

Special gambling houses were set up where people could gamble on cards and dice. Huge sums of money would change hands every evening.

Fencing and shooting were popular. Gentlemen killed each other in duels with swords or pistols, fought over an insult or quarrel.

Boxing became popular at the start of the 19th century. Young noblemen learned to box, but did not fight in public contests.

In the late 18th century, sea-bathing became fashionable for people who could afford to travel to the coast.

They used "bathing machines" to stop people watching them from the beach.

160

Pirates, highwaymen and smugglers

During the 18th century, traders and explorers on long sea trips were likely to be attacked by bands of pirates, who sailed the seas looking for ships to plunder. The West Indies, where many pirates hid among the islands, was an especially dangerous area.

Travel by land was slow, uncomfortable and dangerous. The roads were not made up and coaches sometimes overturned.

There were highwaymen too, who held up the coaches and demanded the passengers' money and valuables.

European countries charged taxes, called customs duties, on goods brought into the country. To avoid paying taxes, smugglers worked secretly, often at night, bringing brandy, silks and other expensive goods from ships moored off the shore.

Towns and villages along the coast had Coast Guards and Excise Officers whose job it was to look out for smugglers. Once on shore the goods had to be hidden until they could be sold. You can still find old inns with secret cellars where smuggled goods were hidden.

When countries such as Britain and France were at war, trade between them was supposed to stop, but the smugglers went on carrying the goods and made great profits. If they were caught they were severely punished and sometimes even hung.

A revolution in farming

In the 18th century, farming methods in England changed completely. The experiments of a few enthusiastic landowners led to the invention of new tools, the introduction of new crops and new ways of improving the soil and breeding better animals. Landowners found it easier to introduce improvements if they gave each farmer a block of land, instead of thin strips in different fields as was usual then. These changes, known as the "Agricultural Revolution", later happened in other parts of Europe.

By using only their best animals for breeding, farmers produced much bigger, healthier animals.

New crops, like turnips and clover were stored in barns, so animals could now be kept and fed over the winter instead of being killed.

Most villagers cannot produce enough food for themselves, now that the common land had been divided up. They have sold their land and now work for other farmers for wages.

Clergyman's house

Village inn

Hedges were planted round the fields.

The village green was all that was left of the old common (land which could be used by all the villagers).

The landowner built these cottages for villagers who work for him.

Vegetable plot

162

Village windmill for grinding corn.

House of chief landowner of the village, often called the squire. Some other villagers owned their land, but he still owned the most.

On pages 104 and 105, you can see what this village looked like in the Middle Ages.

Seed drill sows seeds in straight lines.

New plough cuts deeper furrows.

This carrier delivered goods to the house.

Doctor's house

Ditch for draining land that used to be too wet for growing crops.

Animal manure was spread on the land to make it more fertile.

Landowner (squire)

Blacksmith

This farmer owns the land he farms.

Village shop

Families left to find work in towns.

Milkmaid

Woman spinning

Landowner's wife

Hoeing kept the crops free of weeds so there would be a bigger harvest.

This man rented a farm from the landowner.

In this field, the farmer grew wheat one year, turnips the next, barley the third year and clover the fourth. This order of growing crops kept the field fertile. Fields were no longer left unplanted every third year.

Machines and factories

In the first half of the 18th century, most people in Britain still lived and worked in the countryside. Woollen and cotton cloth, produced in the north of England, were the chief manufactured goods, mainly made by hand, in people's homes. But by 1850, it was being made by machines in factories. The new factories employed lots of people and towns quickly grew up round them. These changes have become known as the "Industrial Revolution".

Britain produced a great deal of woollen cloth. In the first half of the 18th century, most of it was made in people's homes and sold to visiting merchants.

Then machines like these were invented. They helped spinners and weavers to work faster. They were adapted to be driven by water, and then by steam.

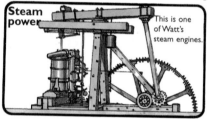

This is one of Watt's steam engines.

The early factories used water power to drive their machines. Various people experimented with the idea of using steam. A Scotsman, James Watt, discovered how to make steam engines drive the wheels of other machines. These were soon used in factories.

Iron was needed for making new machines, but iron-smelting needed charcoal, and the wood for making this was in short supply. Coal fumes made iron brittle. Abraham Darby discovered coal could be turned into coke which was pure enough to make iron.

People had been using coal to heat their homes for a long time, but it had only been dug from shallow mines.

The invention of safety lamps, steam pumps to prevent floods and machines to suck out stale air, made deep mines possible.

Underground rails made it easier to haul coal from great depths. Small children were used to pull the heavy trucks.

Men with money built factories and bought machines to put in them. People working at home could not compete with the prices of factory-made goods, so had to go and work in factories. Many country people could make more money working in factories than on the land.

Drive-wheel transfers power from steam engine to spinning machines.

Leather belts attach drive-wheels to machines.

Factory owner showing visitors round.

Machines for spinning cotton.

Boy climbing into machine to mend it.

Exhausted children often fall asleep at work and are punished.

Women change the bobbins (reels) and watch for breaks in the thread.

Overseer

Machine-smashing

At first, conditions in the factories were very bad. Men, women and children worked very long hours for low wages. Machines had no safety guards and there were bad accidents.

Gradually laws were passed which made the factory owners improve conditions in the factories, made working hours shorter and protected the rights of working people.

Machines were very unpopular with people who had no jobs. Some people even banded together to smash them. One group was called the Luddites after their leader, Ned Ludd.

BRITAIN (THE INDUSTRIAL REVOLUTION):
AD1800 to AD1914
Life in the new towns

Where factories were built, new towns quickly grew up to house the factory workers. They were overcrowded, unhealthy and caused many problems.

Factory owner's house

Factories

Railway (goods line)

Chimney sweep and apprentice

Policeman

BUTCHER

Barrel organ

Hansom cab

Gas lamp

Pickpocket

Fruit-seller

Cheap houses, built back-to-back, were put up for the factory workers. The streets were dirty and the air polluted by factories. Diseases spread quickly. Until cheap ways of travelling were developed the workers had to live near the factories.

166

The changes in farming and industry left some people without jobs. To get help they had to live in "workhouses". Conditions there were harsh to discourage lazy people from using them. Men and women lived in separate quarters so families were split up.

Several reformers tried to help poor people. Dr Barnado, shown here, set up children's homes and General Booth started a Christian organization called the Salvation Army.

Many laws were passed during the 19th century to clean up towns, building better houses and setting up schools where children could go without paying.

Old-age pensions started in 1909. People collected theirs from the post office. In 1911, a law was passed which insured people against sickness and unemployment.

Workers began to form trade unions so that they could bargain for better wages and working conditions by threatening to strike. At first, trade unions were illegal but gradually laws were passed which made them legal. This gave them the right to picket (stand outside their work places and try to persuade other workers not to go in).

Some trade union supporters formed the Labour Party. In the general election of 1906, 29 of their members were elected to Parliament.

167

Transport and travel

The Industrial Revolution brought about immense changes in transport and travel. Some important developments happened first in Britain, others happened first in America and other parts of Europe.

1. In England, companies called Turnpike Trusts were set up. They built and repaired roads and charged people tolls for using them. This is one of the tollgates. Engineers, like Telford and MacAdam, found ways of building roads with hard surfaces.

2. New bridges were also built, many of them iron. This is the Clifton Suspension Bridge in England, designed by Brunel, a famous engineer.

3. Bicycles were in general use by the 1880s. Early "penny-farthings" were ridden by men, but later models were suitable for women too.

4. As the population increased during the 19th century, cities grew in size and people had to live further from their work. Horse-drawn buses were introduced to provide them with transport. Before long, city streets became packed with traffic.

5. The first motor cars were made in Germany in 1885. Until the 1920s, only the very wealthy could afford them.

Canals

In the 18th century, it was cheaper to send heavy goods by water than by road. Where there were no suitable rivers, canals were cut. Locks took boats up and down slopes. Barges were pulled by horses walking along the "towpath".

In 1869, the Suez Canal, which links the Mediterranean Sea to the Red Sea, was opened. This canal cut several weeks off the journey from Europe to India. In 1915, the Panama Canal was opened linking the Atlantic and Pacific Oceans.

Railways

Early type of locomotive designed by famous railway engineer, George Stephenson.

The first steam locomotive to run on rails was built in England in 1804 by Richard Trevithick. Twenty years later, the first passenger railway was opened. Railways became popular. They were a quick, cheap and safe way of carrying people and goods. As train services improved, ordinary people could go on seaside and countryside holidays. England's roads and canals were neglected.

The first stretch of underground railway was built in 1863. Until 1890, when electric trains came in, underground trains were steam-powered and filled the tunnels with soot.

Sea travel

Very fast sailing ships called "clippers" were built during the 19th century and carried light cargoes, such as tea. A completely new kind of ship was also developed at this time. These ships were built of iron and had steam-engines. They gradually replaced sailing ships.

Many lighthouses were built and a lifeboat service introduced, making sea travel much safer than it had been in the past.

Faster and safer sea travel tempted wealthy people to take holidays abroad. In 1869, Thomas Cook ran his first holiday tour to Egypt.

The first flights

The Wright brothers' glider

The Montgolfier brothers were the first to send people into the air, in their hot-air balloon in 1783.

In the early 20th century, the Wright brothers built a glider. They built an aeroplane with an engine and in 1903, made the first powered flight.

Key dates

AD1663/1770	Turnpike trusts set up.
AD1783	First ascent of hot-air balloon.
AD1804	First steam vehicle to run on rails.
AD1829	First railroads opened in U.S.A.
AD1839	First pedal bicycle made.
AD1863	Opening of first underground railway.
AD1869	Suez Canal opened.
AD1885	**Karl Benz** made a 3-wheeled motor car.
AD1886	**Gottlieb Daimler** made a 4-wheeled motor car.
AD1903	First powered flight.

French Revolution and Napoleon's wars

1. The King of France, Louis XVI and his wife, Marie Antoinette, lived in the palace of Versailles, near Paris. They were surrounded by nobles who hardly paid any taxes. Louis was not a good ruler and they were all unpopular with the people.

2. Many nobles were arrogant and treated everyone else with scorn. This annoyed the middle classes.

3. The peasants paid taxes to the church, the government and their local lord, as well as working for their lord.

Execution by guillotine

4. By 1789, the government had no money left, so the king was forced to call a meeting of the States General (parliament), which had not met for 175 years. Later, the States General passed many reforms but most people were still not satisfied.

5. In 1789, a crowd in Paris captured a royal prison called the Bastille. This sparked off riots all over France.

6. The revolution became violent. The king, queen, nobles and anyone not revolutionary enough were executed.

7. European rulers were horrified by events in France. Soon the French were at war with most of the rest of Europe. Many officers were recruited into the French army, in particular Napoleon Bonaparte.

8. Napoleon was a successful military commander. He became First Consul and then Emperor.

9. He conquered much of Europe and made his brothers and sisters rulers. This map shows the lands ruled by him and his family by 1810.

10. Napoleon planned to invade Britain, his most determined enemy. But after the British defeated the French at sea in the Battle of Trafalgar, he gave up the idea.

11. In 1812, Napoleon invaded Russia with an army of 600,000 men. He defeated the Tsar's army and marched to Moscow. But the Russians had set fire to Moscow and removed all the provisions. This shows the French army returning home in the middle of winter. Hundreds of thousands of them died from cold and hunger.

12. After his disastrous invasion of Russia, there was a reaction against Napoleon in Europe. British troops helped the Spanish drive the French out of Spain.

The Battle of Waterloo

The Battle of Waterloo was the last great battle in the wars against Napoleon. The French were completely defeated by a British army, led by Wellington and a Prussian army, led by Blücher.

Louis XVIII was made King of France. Napoleon was imprisoned on the small British island of St Helena in the South Atlantic Ocean, where he died in 1821.

Key dates

AD1789	First meeting of the States General.
AD1792	France went to war with Austria and Prussia.
AD1793/1794	Period called the "Reign of Terror". Hundreds of people guillotined.
AD1804	**Napoleon** became Emperor.
AD1805	Battle of Trafalgar.
AD1808/1814	War between the British and French in Spain and Portugal.
AD1812	**Napoleon's** invasion of Russia.
AD1815	Battle of Waterloo.

171

New nations and ways of governing

The 18th and 19th centuries were times of great change in the way countries were governed. There were many revolutions and several new, independent nations emerged.

Independence for America

1. Most European settlers in America lived in the 13 colonies* on the east coast. In the early 18th century, Britain helped them in the wars against the Native North Americans and the French. The British taxed the settlers to pay for the wars. Sometimes, the settlers attacked British tax officers.

2. In 1775, war broke out. The British Army was far from home. The settlers were on their own ground and their riflemen were good shots.

3. In 1781, the British surrendered. In 1783, they signed a treaty recognizing the United States of America as an independent nation.

4. The new constitution (set of rules by which a country is governed) was agreed upon and George Washington was chosen as President.

Key dates

AD1775/1783	War of American Independence.
AD1789/1797	**George Washington** President of the U.S.A.
AD1818/1883	Life of **Karl Marx**.
AD1859/1860	**General Garibaldi** drove French and Austrian out of Italy.
AD1861	Kingdom of Italy founded.
AD1871	German Empire founded. **William I** became Kaiser and **Bismarck** First Chancellor.

Germany

Early in the 19th century, Germany was a group of states, the strongest of which was Prussia. In 1861, William I became King of Prussia. With his chief minister, Bismarck, he gradually brought all Germany under his control. In 1871, William was proclaimed Kaiser (emperor) of Germany.

Battleship being launched

Germany became very strong. It quickly built a large navy, developed industries and won colonies in Africa and the Far East.

Germans became interested in their own history. The operas of Wagner, based on tales of German gods and heroes, became popular.

Italy

In Italy, some states were independent and some were ruled by Austria. General Garibaldi and his soldiers, known as the "Red Shirts", shown, helped to drive the foreigners out of Italy and make it an independent nation.

ITALY IN 1866

GERMAN EMPIRE IN 1871

Ideas about government

1. In Britain, people chose which political party should rule by voting at elections. At first, few people could vote but it was extended to all men.

2. Some women began to demand the right to vote. They were called suffragettes. They held marches and caused as much disturbance as possible to win support.

3. Rulers were afraid of democracy (people having a say in running of country). They used soldiers against people who protested.

4. Sometimes people with revolutionary ideas were executed or put in prison so they could not lead the people against their ruler.

5. Some people believed any form of government was wrong. They were called anarchists and they killed many political leaders.

6. A German thinker, called Karl Marx, wrote many books with new ideas about government. He wanted people to get rid of their rulers in a revolution and then have new governments run by the working people. Communism is based on his ideas.

173

Slavery and civil war

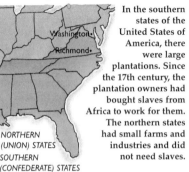

In the southern states of the United States of America, there were large plantations. Since the 17th century, the plantation owners had bought slaves from Africa to work for them. The northern states had small farms and industries and did not need slaves.

NORTHERN (UNION) STATES

SOUTHERN (CONFEDERATE) STATES

1. The slave trade became well organized. Europeans captured Africans or bought them from local rulers.

2. Conditions on slave ships to America were awful. The more slaves a trader got on a ship, the greater his profit.

3. When they reached America, slaves who had survived the voyage were sold at auctions. They could be sold again, so families were often separated.

4. Slaves were lucky if they worked in their master's house, but most were used as field hands on the plantation. Most estate owners grew cotton, tobacco or sugar, all of which need constant attention. Because of the heat, African slaves were thought best for this work. Some masters were cruel but others treated their slaves quite well.

5. Many slaves tried to escape to the north where there was no slavery. A black woman, Harriet Tubman, helped 19 groups of slaves escape.

6. Protests against slavery grew. In 1833 slavery was abolished in the British Empire. The Anti-Slavery Society was founded in America. This is its badge.

7. In American Congress there were bitter arguments about slavery. Northerners wanted to abolish it but southerners were determined to keep slaves.

The outbreak of war

In 1861, the southern states elected their own president and broke away from the Union of the United States, declaring themselves a "confederacy". The north thought the states should stay united so war broke out between the Unionists (northerners) and Confederates (southerners). It lasted for four years. There were many fierce battles and nearly 635,000 people lost their lives.

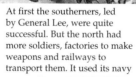

Camp

Mine exploding

Southern (Confederate) flag

Northern (Unionist) flag

Barbed wire

Trench

A new style of fighting developed during the American Civil War. Soldiers made trenches protected by barbed wire. They used hand-grenades, mines and flame throwers.

At first the southerners, led by General Lee, were quite successful. But the north had more soldiers, factories to make weapons and railways to transport them. It used its navy to stop ships bringing supplies to the south. Despite terrible suffering the southerners fought on bravely, but in 1865 they were finally forced to surrender.

1. President Abraham Lincoln, elected before the war, hoped to make a lasting peace, but he was assassinated at Ford's Theater in Washington.

2. The south had been ruined by the war and its main town, Richmond, had been burned. For years afterwards white and black people were very poor.

3. Some southerners still saw black people as slaves. They formed the Ku Klux Klan, a secret society, and wore sheets and terrorized black people.

Explorers and empire builders

In 1750, there were still huge areas of the world where Europeans had never been. During the late 18th and the 19th centuries, European explorers set out to discover as much as they could about the lands and oceans of the world. Traders and settlers followed and European countries began to set up colonies abroad which they ruled.

Captain Cook

Captain Cook led three expeditions (1768-79) to the Pacific Ocean. He visited islands such as Tahiti where he was met by war canoes.

He explored the east coast of Australia. Its strange animals fascinated the artists and scientists on the expedition.

He also sailed round New Zealand. The crew of his ship *Endeavor* landed and met the Maoris who lived there.

Exploring Africa

1. In the 19th century, people explored and made maps of Africa. They saw sights such as the Victoria Falls, but many fell ill and died of strange diseases.

2. While searching for the Nile, two British explorers, Speke and Grant, stayed with Mutesa, King of Buganda.

3. Explorers, such as Dr Livingstone, were also Christian missionaries* and set up hospitals and schools for the Africans, as well as churches.

4. The Frenchman, René Caillé, was an early European explorer in the Sahara Desert. He was one of the first Europeans to see the ancient city of Timbuktu.

5. There were several women explorers in the 19th century. This is Alexandrine Tinné, a Dutch heiress, who travelled through North Africa and the Sudan.

Other expeditions

1. Richard Burton disguised himself to visit the Arab holy city, Mecca, where only Muslims were allowed.

2. Many explorers never returned from the jungles of South America where they went to make maps and search for lost cities.

3. Later explorers travelled to the frozen north and south. In 1909, Robert Peary, an American, was the first to reach the North Pole. Roald Amundsen reached the South Pole in 1911.

Setting up colonies

1. Europeans wanted new places to sell their factory-made goods and wanted to buy raw materials such as cotton and tea.

2. If quarrels between local rulers threatened trade, Europeans sent armies, which often stayed after the fighting was over.

3. They sent officials to organize and govern the territory for them, thus setting up colonies.

4. More and more Europeans went to the colonies and settled there with their families. They organized vast estates where local people worked and grew tea, rubber, cotton and foodstuffs or reared sheep and cattle. When minerals were discovered, factories and railways were built and still more people went to live in the colonies.

5. In Europe, politicians were worried by the increase in population and encouraged people to settle in the colonies where there was land and work.

Europeans in Africa

North Africa

1. In the early 19th century, most of the countries in North Africa were part of the Ottoman Empire*, which was breaking up, so European powers began to move in. The French gained control of Algeria, Tunisia and Morocco. Here, tribesmen are attacking a French fort, defended by the French Foreign Legion.

2. The Egyptian ruler needed money, so he sold his shares in the Suez Canal to Britain. Britain became involved in Egyptian affairs and took over government.

3. Egypt ruled the Sudan. In 1883, a religious leader, the Mahdi, led a revolt. Britain sent an army led by General Gordon, but it was defeated at Khartoum.

Trading in the west

These gold objects were made by the Ashanti people of West Africa, who grew rich trading in gold and slaves. They fought the British, but were defeated.

Zimbabwe

Zimbabwe was the capital city of a rich African kingdom. It was destroyed probably in the early 19th century by a rival tribe.

South Africa

Dutch settlers arrived in South Africa in 1652. They set up Cape Colony on the Cape of Good Hope. They became known as "Boers" (Dutch word for farmers). In 1814, an international treaty gave Cape Colony to the British. The Boers hated being ruled by the British and between 1835 and 1837 many set off north, with their possessions in wagons, to find lands free from British rule. This movement is called the "Great Trek".

Cecil Rhodes

Cecil Rhodes made a fortune from diamond and gold mines, then formed a company to build a railway from the British colony to the mining area north of the Boer states. In 1895, this area became known as Rhodesia.

The Grab for Africa

■	FRENCH
■	BRITISH
■	GERMAN
■	PORTUGUESE
■	BELGIAN
■	SPANISH
☐	ITALIAN

In 1880, much of Africa was still independent of any European country. This map shows how the European powers carved up nearly the whole of Africa between them, between 1880 and 1914.

The Boers came into conflict with the Zulus, the fiercest of the neighbouring African tribes. The British helped the Boers and in 1879, defeated the Zulus.

The British increased their control over the Boer states. In 1886, gold was discovered and more British people came to work in them.

In 1899, war broke out between the Boers and the British. The Boers did well at first. They rode fast horses and were good at stalking their enemy.

The British destroyed the Boers' farms and animals, and put all the Boers they could find, including women and children, into special prison camps. In 1902, the Boers surrendered.

Key dates

AD1814	Britain gained control of Cape Colony.
c.AD1830	Collapse of Kingdom of Zimbabwe.
AD1830	French began to take over North Africa.
AD1835/1837	The Great Trek.
AD1875	Britain bought Egypt's shares in the Suez Canal.
AD1878/9	Zulu War.
AD1885	Fall of Khartoum.
AD1896	Britain took over Matabeleland which became Rhodesia.
AD1899/1902	Boer War.
AD1901	Ashanti kingdom became British.
AD1910	Union of South Africa set up.

The British in India

1. The British East India Company started as a trading company. By the 19th century it governed most of India.

2. The British tried to modernize India, but also tried to stop some of the Indians' customs. The Indians resented this. In 1857 some *sepoys* (Indian soldiers in the British Army) mutinied. The British regained control but in future, they made more careful changes.

3. After the Mutiny, the East India Company lost its right to rule. The British Government appointed its own officials. Indian princes lost their power but were still wealthy and lived in luxury.

4. Queen Victoria became Empress of India in 1876. Many Indians felt this created a special tie with Britain.

5. The British brought their own customs to India. They introduced cricket which became one of the national sports of India.

6. Indian cities were poor and crowded. Disease and famine were common. Improvements could be made only slowly.

7. The two main religious groups in India were Hindus and Muslims. They were rivals. Sometimes people were killed in riots.

8. The Indians had little say in how their country was ruled. A group formed the National Congress. At first they just wanted reforms but later they began to demand independence from Britain.

Convicts and settlers

1. In 1788, the British began to send criminals to Australia as punishment. Many stayed on after they had served their sentence.

2. Soon other settlers arrived. Most wanted land where they could raise sheep and cattle. Some went in search of gold and minerals.

3. 19th century life in Australia was hard and dangerous. There were "bushrangers" (outlaws). The most famous was Ned Kelly.

4. Settlers took land from the Aborigines (native Australians), many of whom were killed or died of diseases brought by settlers.

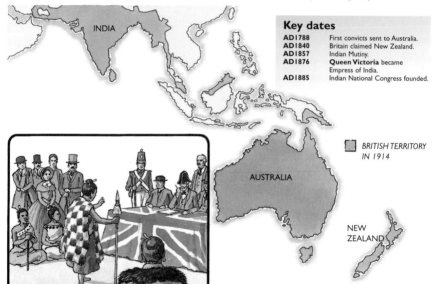

Key dates

AD1788	First convicts sent to Australia.
AD1840	Britain claimed New Zealand.
AD1857	Indian Mutiny.
AD1876	**Queen Victoria** became Empress of India.
AD1885	Indian National Congress founded.

INDIA

BRITISH TERRITORY IN 1914

AUSTRALIA

NEW ZEALAND

5. European settlers first arrived in New Zealand in the 1790s. In 1840, the British Government took over the country. The Governor and the Maori chiefs made a treaty agreeing how much land the settlers could have, but this did not prevent fierce wars between the Maoris and the settlers.

This map shows British territory in India, South-East Asia and Australia in 1914. By this time, Australia and New Zealand had gained the right to rule themselves, but they were still part of the British Empire.

Native North Americans and settlers

There were many tribes of Native North Americans, each with its own way of life and language. On the Great Plains, they lived by farming, until they captured horses from the Spaniards in the 16th century. Then most of them became nomads, hunting buffalo and rearing horses. They lived like this for about 200 years, until European settlers moved west and took the Native North Americans' hunting grounds for their farms.

Buffalo hunt. The buffalo provided Indians with food, clothing and shelter.

Tepee (tent made of buffalo hide)

Chiefs

Meat drying

Traders

Travois (sledge)

Preparing buffalo hide

Part of this tepee wall has been removed so you can see inside.

Medicine man

The Plains Americans lived in tepees which could be packed up when the buffalo moved on. The first white men to meet them were traders who sold metal goods, blankets and guns, and bought buffalo hides and horses.

Settlers move west

As European settlers moved into the original 13 colonies of America, more land was needed. In 1803, the Americans bought Louisiana from the French.

Settlers began to cross the Appalachian Mountains and the Great Plains, looking for land to farm. They travelled with wagons packed with everything they needed for their new homes. Most people, except for guards and cattle herders had to walk. It usually took many months to reach a suitable area.

California
GREAT PLAINS
Louisiana
APPALACHIAN MOUNTAINS

UNITED STATES OF AMERICA IN 1783

Settlers made treaties with the Native Americans not to take their land, but broke these treaties when they needed land.

Gold was discovered in California, in 1848. Thousands of people flocked there in the "goldrush", hoping to make fortunes.

Railways were built to link the east and west coasts. These brought more settlers to the Great Plains, leaving less land for Natives.

The men who built the tracks had to be fed. They employed hunters to kill the buffalo on which Natives depended.

Native Americans fought the settlers in bitter wars and won victories, such as at Little Big Horn, where they killed General Custer and his men. But, the settlers had more soldiers and better weapons. Many Native tribes were almost wiped out.

Native Americans were left with small areas of land called reservations, controlled by government agents. Most were unhappy.

The Wild West

In the United States of America, many of the people who moved to the vast plains and prairies started raising cattle or growing corn. Towns grew up to supply their needs. At first, they were wild, lawless places, especially when cowboys came into town. They brought herds of cattle to railway depots, which were taken to feed people in cities.

Large industries and cities like New York and Chicago grew up. The first skyscrapers were built. By 1890, the United States was one of the world's most powerful industrial nations.

Farmers on the plains started using tougher crops and steel ploughs. They bought machines for harvesting and threshing. Before long, they were producing vast quantities of grain which were sold all over the world.

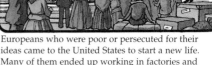

Europeans who were poor or persecuted for their ideas came to the United States to start a new life. Many of them ended up working in factories and living in hard conditions in the big cities.

New countries in South America

Revolutionary leader, Simon Bolivar.

Between 1810 and 1825, a series of revolutions ended Portuguese and Spanish rule in South America. 11 new states were set up.

Coffee was brought from Arabia to South America. By 1860, it was the main export of many states.

Jungle

SOUTH AMERICA

Pampas

Another important export was rubber. It was made from the juice of trees growing in the Amazon jungle.

Many of the Indian tribes in the Amazon jungle attacked the white men who came to take over their lands.

On the pampas (grasslands), there were ranches where cowboys called "gauchos", reared great herds of cattle.

The cattle were used for making canned meat which was sold abroad.

Mexico

Americans and Mexicans quarrelled about who should control Texas. It belonged to Mexico but many Americans settled there. Here Davy Crockett and some Americans are defending the Alamo Fort against Mexican attack.

In 1867, Mexicans shot Maximilian dead.

Europe tried to control Mexico and made Maximilian of Austria, Emperor of Mexico.

From 1867 onwards, the Mexicans ruled themselves. In the early 20th century civil war broke out. One of the revolutionary leaders was Pancho Villa, shown here.

Life under the Tsars

The Tsars (emperors) of Russia governed their huge country from St Petersburg. There was no parliament. The Tsars and nobles, from whom they chose ministers and officials, were cut off from the rest of the country. Much of their time was spent at balls and receptions.

Most Russians were Orthodox Christians, who supported the idea that the Tsar was chosen by God and that he alone had the right to rule.

It was forbidden to write or talk about government reforms. Secret police tracked down anyone suspected of wanting to change the government.

People who criticized the government for its inefficiency and cruelty, were executed or sent into exile in a part of Russia called Siberia.

In the 19th century, there were several great novelists, playwrights and composers in Russia. The Russian ballet became world-famous.

Many Russians were serfs (peasants who lived on nobles' estates and were treated as slaves). Serfs were bought and sold. They had to do any work their estate owner demanded and were often given punishments for small mistakes. There were frequent uprisings and riots. In 1861, Tsar Alexander II freed the serfs. The government lent them money to buy land, but they were too poor to buy farming equipment and pay back the loans. Many were worse off than before.

The Crimean War

AUSTRIAN EMPIRE
CRIMEA — RUSSIAN EMPIRE
TURKISH EMPIRE
BLACK SEA

The Russians wanted to expand their empire. They expanded eastwards and also won land around the Black Sea, by helping these people free themselves from the Turkish Empire. In 1853, Britain and France tried to capture the area called the Crimea, to stop Russian expansion. One incident in this war was the Charge of the Light Brigade (shown here). A British force misunderstood an order and charged the Russian guns.

Discontent grows

1. Nicholas II became Tsar in 1894. He was a well-meaning and kind man, but he was not strong enough to be a good ruler.

2. Nicholas's wife, Alexandra, was under the spell of Rasputin, a monk. She thought he could cure her son of a blood disease. Others thought him evil.

3. Factories and industrial towns were growing up in Russia. Living conditions were bad and people started demanding changes.

4. In 1905, some workers went on strike and marched to the Tsar to tell him their problems. Fearing revolution, soldiers fired on them.

5. The Tsar allowed a *Duma* (parliament) to meet for a while, but a group of people in exile, led by Lenin, were planning a revolution.

Key dates

AD1762/1796	Reign of **Catherine the Great**.
AD1812	Invasion of Russia by Napoleon.
AD1853/1856	Crimean War.
AD1855/1881	Reign of **Alexander II**.
AD1861	Serfs freed.
AD1885	Fall of Khartoum.
AD1894/1917	Reign of **Nicholas II**.
AD1904/1905	Russia defeated in war with Japan.
AD1905	Massacre of strikers outside Tsar's palace.
AD1906	Meeting of Duma (parliament).

Western ideas in the East

Japan

Last Japanese Shogun

From about 1640 onwards, Japan had no contact with the countries of the west, except for a few Dutch traders. Then, in 1853, Commodore Perry, the commander of a squadron of American warships, sailed to Japan. Soon European powers followed and Japan made trade agreements with many European countries.

It was hundreds of years since any emperor of Japan had had any real power. An official, called the Shogun, ruled the country for the emperor.

The Emperor arriving in Edo

In 1868, the 15-year old Emperor left the old capital, Kyoto and set up a new one in Edo (Tokyo).

In Edo, he took power from the Shogun and set up a western-style parliament.

The small picture above shows the opening of the first parliament.

The Samurai (warriors) were replaced by a new army. They were trained in modern methods of fighting by advisers from France and Germany.

The Japanese learnt much from the west. They built railways and factories and started producing large numbers of goods quickly and cheaply.

The Japanese wanted to win power overseas. They started to interfere in China and Korea. This made them rivals with the Russians and in 1904, Japan and Russia went to war. The new efficient Japanese army and navy quickly defeated the Russians.

China

From 1644 to 1912, China was ruled by the Ch'ing (also called the Manchu) Emperors. This is Ch'ien Lung (1736-95).

Ch'ing emperors fought wars to protect their frontiers, win territory and put down rebellions. At first, they were successful but the wars were expensive. Later emperors found it difficult to pay for them and the country became weaker.

The population was growing but farming methods were old-fashioned. There was not enough food for everyone.

The Chinese Government did not like foreigners and only allowed them to trade in certain areas. The British were keen to extend these areas, so in 1839 they went to war.

In 1842, the British won the war. They forced the Chinese to sign a treaty which gave them Hong Kong and allowed them to trade in other ports.

Some Chinese decided to strengthen China by adopting Western ideas and inventions, such as railways and steamships. But many hated foreign ideas.

People who hated foreigners formed a secret society called the "Boxers". In 1900, they started attacking all the foreigners they could find in China. Here they are storming a foreign embassy.

Empress Tzu Hsi ruled China from 1862 to 1908, first for her son, then for her nephew. She plotted with those who hated foreigners.

In 1911, there was a revolution and the last Ch'ing Emperor was expelled from China. This is Sun Yat-sen the first President of China.

Time Chart

Dark Ages to 1914

	North America	Central and South America	Europe	Africa
	Mound Builders living on the plains.		Gradual conversion of barbarian kingdoms to Christianity.	North Africa and Egypt part of the Byzantine Empire.
			Invasion of Spain by Muslims. Battle of Poitiers. Muslim advance into Western Europe halted.	North Africa and Egypt overrun by Muslim Arabs.
AD800		Decline of Maya civilisation in Mexico.	Viking raids begin. **Charlemagne** crowned Holy Roman Emperor.	Various tribes start living south of the Sahara Desert.
AD900				
AD1000	Vikings may have reached America.		Normans invade England. Normans invade Italy. First Crusade.	First Iron Age settlement at Zimbabwe.
AD1100		Chimu people living in Peru.		Zimbabwe becomes a powerful kingdom.
AD1200			The Mongols invade Eastern Europe. Eighth Crusade.	Arab merchants known to be trading in West and East Africa.
AD1300			Beginning of Hundred Years War. Black Death from Asia spreads through Europe. First firearms developed.	Rise of Empire of Mali in West Africa.
AD1400	People living at Huff.	Rise of Aztec Empire in Mexico.	Invention of printing. Ideas of Renaissance spreading from Italy. European explorers discover America.	Chinese merchants trading in East Africa. Kingdom of Benin set up. Portuguese expeditions explore west coast and start trading with Africans.
AD1500	Voyage of Christopher Columbus.	Spread of Inca Empire in Peru. Arrival of Spaniards. End of Aztec and Inca Empires.	Beginning of Reformation. Wars of Religion between Catholics and Protestants.	Turks conquered Egypt. Mali Empire destroyed. Beginning of slave trade.
AD 1600	Spaniards brought horses to America. First European settlements. Pilgrim Fathers arrive in New England.	Arrival of Portuguese.	Development of trade between Europe and other parts of the world. English Civil War.	Dutch settlers arrive in South Africa.
AD1700	England wins Canada from French. War of American Independence.		Beginning of Agricultural Revolution in Britain. Beginning of Industrial Revolution in Britain.	Rise of Ashanti power on west coast.
AD1800	United States buys Louisiana from the French. California goldrush.	Spaniards and Portuguese driven out of Central and South America.	French Revolution. Wars of **Napoleon**. Unification of Italy. Unification of Germany.	Slave trade abolished within British Empire. The Great Trek. Opening of Suez Canal.
AD1900	American Civil War.	Mexican Revolution begins.	World War I.	European powers build up empires in Africa. Boer war begins. Union of South Africa established.

Russia and Asia	Middle East	India	China and Japan	Far East and Pacific
Slavs in Russia	Byzantine Empire controls much of Middle East. Death of **Muhammad**. Spread of Muslim Empire. Muslims conquer much of Byzantine Empire.	India ruled by many princes.	T'ang Dynasty in China.	
Muslims conquer Persia.				
			Japanese capital moved to Kyoto.	
Vikings settle in Russia.				Rise of the Khmers in Cambodia. First settlers reach Easter Island and New Zealand from Polynesia.
Kiev becomes officially Christian.				
Russia becomes officially Christian.	Seljuk Turks invade Byzantine Empire.		Sung Dynasty in China.	
	Invasion of Seljuk Turks.			
	The First Crusade.			
	Kingdom of Outremer founded. Life of **Saladin**.		Appearance of Samurai in Japan. Military rulers in Japan take the title "Shogun".	Large statues erected on Easter Island.
	Sack of Constantinople by Crusaders.			
Mongols invade and conquer Russia.	End of kingdom of Outremer.		**Marco Polo** visits China. The Mongol ruler, **Kublai Khan**, conquers China.	
			Ming Dynasty in China.	
		Mongols invade northern India.		
Rise of Moscow. Russia gradually united. **Ivan III** becomes first Tsar and throws off Mongol power.	Sack of Constantinople by Ottoman Turks. End of Byzantine Empire.	First European sea voyage to India and back, led by **Vasco da Gama** (Portuguese).	Long period of war in Japan.	Europeans first see Pacific Ocean.
Rise of Safavid Dynasty in Persia. **Tsar Ivan the Terrible**. Development of trade between Russia and England.	**Suleiman the Magnificent**. Turks threaten Europe. Turkish advance into Europe halted.	Mogul Empire set up.	Arrival in Japan and China of European traders and missionaries.	First Europeans cross the Pacific Ocean on their way round the world.
		British start regular trade with India.	All Europeans, except Dutch traders, expelled from Japan. The Manchu family start the Ch'ing Dynasty in China.	Expansion of Dutch trade in East Indies.
Tsar Peter the Great.	Europeans try to extend their trade with Turkey and Persia.	British destroy French trade with India.		Dutch land in Australia. **Captain Cook** reaches Australia and New Zealand. British colony of Australia founded.
Napoleon's expedition to Moscow. Crimean War. **Nicholas II** becomes Tsar. Meeting of the First Duma (parliament).	Ottoman Empire falling apart. Russia tries to help parts of Empire break free. World War I.	Britain gradually gains control of the whole of India. Indian Mutiny. **Queen Victoria** proclaimed Empress of India.	War between the British and Chinese. **Commodore Perry** arrives in Japan. Boxer uprising in China. War between Japan and Russia. Revolution in China. Last Ch'ing Emperor expelled.	Britain takes possession of New Zealand. French build up empire in Indo-China.

Index

Consultant editors

Brian Adams, D. Barass, Professor Edmund Bosworth, Ben Burt, Dr Warwick Bray, Elizabeth Carter,
Mark Hassall, Amelie Kuhrt, Dr M.C. Chapman, T.R. Clayton, Norman Hampson, George Hart,
Dr C.J. Heywood, Dr Alan Johnston, Peter Johnson, Dr Michael Loewe, Dr M. McCauley, Dr Roger Moorey,
Dr J.A. Sharpe, Dr C.D. Sheldon, R.W. Skelton, Margaret Somerville, Joanna Strub, Dr R. Waller.